The Building Blocks of
FREE=MOTION
QUILTING

D1604703

Published in 2020
by Lucky Spool Media, LLC

www.luckyspool.com

5424 Sunol Blvd., Suite 10-118
Pleasanton, CA 94566, USA

info@luckyspool.com

Text © Kathleen Riggins
Editor: Susanne Woods
Designer: Page + Pixel
Photographer: Page + Pixel
Illustrator: Kari Vojtechovsky

All rights reserved. No part of this book may be reproduced in
any form or by any means, electronic, or mechanical, including
photocopying, recording, or by any information storage and
retrieval system without permission in writing from the publisher.
Trademarked names (™) and ® are used throughout the book with
no intention of infringement and to benefit the legal owner. Lucky
Spool Media and associated logos are trademarked by Lucky Spool
Media, LLC.

The information in this book is accurate and complete to the best of
our knowledge. All recommendations are made without guarantee
on the part of the author or Lucky Spool Media, LLC. The author and
publisher disclaim any liability in connection with this information.

The patterns in this book are copyrighted and must not be made
for resale.

9 8 7 6 5 4 3 2 1
First Edition

Printed in China

Library of Congress Cataloging-in-Publication
Data available upon request

978-1-940655-42-0
LSID0052

The Building Blocks of FREE-MOTION QUILTING

Combining 8 Easy Designs Into Knock-Out Custom Quilting

Kathleen Riggins

TABLE OF CONTENTS

INTRduction

It's our opportunity, as quilters, to add our own personality to a quilt. We often follow patterns and use fabrics designed by someone else...but in the quilting, we add our own flavor.

This book came about because of my own limitations. I just don't like very many quilting designs. Because of this, I've learned ways to use the ones I love in as many ways as I can think of. And now, I am going to share them with you.

Quilting is the best part of making a quilt. Clearly.

I split this book into three parts. First, we learn to quilt some of my favorite basic designs that I used in my book and in most of my quilts. This way, we all start at much the same place.

Next, we talk about ways to combine the designs together. I split this section into design categories, so we learn three ways to combine a design with other designs. Then, for each of those three combinations, I share two ways to use that combination method with other designs. Altogether, that's 57 ways to combine designs!

Finally, we take a more structured approach and look at different shapes we can make with our quilting and the combinations we learned in the previous sections.

I think that's enough preamble… let's get ready to quilt!

SET IT UP

MACHINE SET UP

Setting your machine up properly for free-motion quilting makes a huge difference in how much you enjoy the process. When I first started free-motion quilting, I often got so frustrated I just wanted to throw my machine out the window. Here are some tips for making your own quilting space just perfect for the adventure we are about to go on.

Extension Table and Sewing Table

I quilt using a 24″ × 18″ Plexiglas extension table fitted for my machine and set up on the biggest table in my house. The extension table provides a large, smooth surface in addition to the bed of my machine, which makes it easy to manipulate my quilts as I work on them. Sometimes, I rearrange half the furniture in my house so I not only have a table in front of me with my machine on it, but I also have a table to my left side. This allows the tables to hold the full weight of the quilt and also makes it easier to move. The tables holding all that weight also prevent stress on my shoulders and arms as I work.

Something I've recently started doing (and have had great luck with) is pushing my machine further back on my table than I used to. If I leave between six and eight inches of table in front of my machine, my posture is good, because I can easily see my needle without slouching, and I can keep my arms further from my body, which helps my shoulders and arms from tensing up.

Machine Needles

When free-motion quilting, use a strong needle. This is because fabric moves differently when free-motion quilting, since the feed dogs aren't engaged as they are when piecing or using a walking foot attachment. Feed dogs stop the fabric from moving while the needle is in the fabric, and they move the fabric when the needle is up. When free-motion quilting, the quilt is moving at a rate determined by your movement, not by your machine. Because of this, sometimes the quilt is being moved when the needle is still down. This causes the needle to flex slightly and isn't good for the stitching or the sewing machine.

I quilt with a size $100/16$ Jeans needle.

Choose a strong needle to prevent needle flex as much as possible. Jeans needles are specifically designed to be stronger than other needles, thus they flex less as the fabric moves. I choose a large size ($^{100}/_{16}$). Why do I care about having less flex? It helps prevent stitch quality issues, such as skipped stitches, tension fluctuation and shredding threads.

Thread manufacturers often recommend needles to give you the best results with their threads. These can be useful recommendations for day-to-day piecing, but they aren't always the best choice for free-motion quilting. If I am frustrated that things aren't working the way I want with the Jeans $^{100}/_{16}$ needle, I try the manufacturer's recommendation. But 90% of the time, I find that the Jeans $^{100}/_{16}$ needle is the best choice.

BASTING YOUR QUILT SANDWICH

Basting a quilt properly makes a huge difference in how well the quilting turns out. Poorly basted quilts often develop puckers and look lumpy. No one wants a lumpy quilt.

My preference is to spray baste. I've been doing this for more than 15 years, and I've never had any issues. Spray baste washes out the first time you wash a quilt, but it holds for as long as you need it to before washing. I have quilts that were spray basted a solid 14 years ago and they are still holding together (that's another story…). I prefer spray over pins for several reasons:

It's easier to baste
No sore fingers from all the pinning or having to tape the backing to the floor to prevent shift.

The quilt is lighter
Without all the pins weighing the quilt down, it is easier to maneuver through my machine.

No moving pins
As there are no pins in the quilt, I don't have to worry about moving them around when they are in the way of my quilting.

Better stabilization
When I spray, every inch of my quilt is basted. When I pin, stabilization is only where the pins are.

My Basting Method

1. Position the batting on a large, smooth surface. (I usually use the floor, but a large table also works.) Smooth your quilt top on top of the batting. **fig. A**

Use newspapers, cardboard, or an old sheet underneath your batting to catch overspray. Spray baste is super annoying to try to wash off floors, trust me.

2. Fold back the quilt top about 10″ along the narrower edge, leaving the batting flat on the floor. Keep folding the quilt top back in 10″ chunks until reaching the middle of the quilt. **fig. B**

3. Spray a section of the batting just above the final fold, the same width as the fold. Hold the spray baste can about 10″ away from the batting. **fig. C**

4. Unfold one roll of the quilt. Starting at the center, smooth the quilt over the sprayed section of batting. Don't pull the fabric tight, but make sure there are no folds or bubbles. **fig. D**

5. Repeat Steps 3 and 4 until reaching the top edge. Rotate the quilt, and baste the other half in the same way.

6. Flip the quilt sandwich over, and repeat the spray-basting process with the backing.

Always spray onto the batting rather than the quilt. This prevents large globs of spray from soaking through your quilt top. While this doesn't hurt your quilt, it can be annoying!

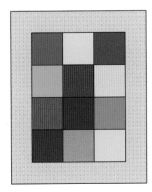

A

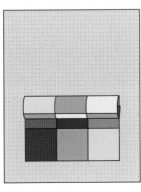

B

C

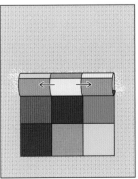

D

MARKING TOOLS

Marking your quilt top with either your entire design or just with dots for reference is the worst. I don't have a magic solution to make it suddenly fun. I often go out of my way to avoid marking, spending far longer trying not to mark than I would have spent marking in the first place. However, sometimes marking is worth it. Throughout this book, I'll always tell you which ones I mark, because it definitely isn't every design I've included in this book!

When I do have to mark, I have four favorite tools.

Hera Marker

This tool is my favorite for certain things. It is great for marking straight lines. You press hard on it, and it creates a crease in the fabric. I love this, because you don't need to take out the marking after quilting. However, it can be difficult to use on certain fabrics, and it doesn't work well for curves.

A Hera marker works great for quilting on a domestic machine but not as well on a longarm, where there is no hard surface under the quilt to help create the crease.

Mechanical Fabric Pencil with White Lead

My next-choice for a marking tool is a white fabric pencil. Non-mechanical pencils are available too, but I prefer the mechanical one as it stays sharp and comes out of my fabric more easily when I'm ready. This creates a thin line that stays on the fabric while I'm quilting but is easy to get out of the fabric later. The one downside is that it is white, so it only shows up on dark fabrics—and to be completely honest, I rarely mark on dark fabrics.

Actually, I never use colored chalk pens to mark my quilt tops. They are extremely difficult to remove and often they won't come out completely. I stick with white and if I need a color other than that, I choose a different marking tool.

Purple Air-Erase Pen

This is the marking tool I use most often. It is temporary, so it doesn't stay on the fabric forever. This pen disappears faster the higher the humidity. For me, in Alberta, it lasts a couple hours in the summer and a couple weeks in the winter. However, I've taught quilting classes in more humid places where the mark barely made it onto the fabric before it was gone. Be aware of how long you need things to last before you mark! I use this for marking an area before I quilt it, but I don't use it to mark a whole quilt or areas I'm not going to be quilting for a while.

Blue Water-Erase Pen

This pen stays in your fabric until it is soaked with water. It's great for marking areas where I want the marking to stay visible for the entire time I am working on a quilt. I use it for marking large shapes over an entire quilt. However, as the quilt needs to be fully submerged in water to remove the markings, I try to limit my use of this pen.

Rulers

I do most of my marking with a regular quilting ruler. I like to use a 4″ × 14″ ruler, as it is small enough to be easily maneuvered around my quilt, but large enough to get the length I usually need.

STARTING AND STOPPING

Trying to keep starts and stops neat and tidy can be tough and annoying. Still, it is an important part of keeping everything looking nice and even when the quilt is finished.

A

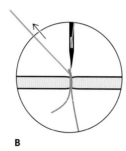

B

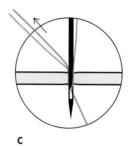

C

Starting

I always start quilting by pulling my threads up to the top of the quilt. This keeps them from tangling on the back or jamming up and creating a big nest.

1. Take a full stitch where the quilting will begin. The needle should go into the fabric then back out. (I usually use the needle up/down button on my sewing machine for this step. If your sewing machine doesn't have this button, I recommend using the hand wheel on the side of your machine.) **fig. A**

2. Pull on the long end of the top thread until the bobbin thread comes up through the top of the quilt. Grab the bobbin thread and pull it all the way through. **fig. B**

3. Holding onto both the top thread and the bobbin thread, stitch a few stitches right on top of one another and start quilting! Once reaching a few inches away from the start, snip off the thread tails. **fig. C**

I prefer to cut my thread tails as opposed to burying them for 95% of my quilts. The only exception I make is if I am making a quilt specifically for a big show. Then, I bury most of my threads. For quilts that I know will be used frequently, however, I tack those stitches down with a few more on top of them, and away I go!

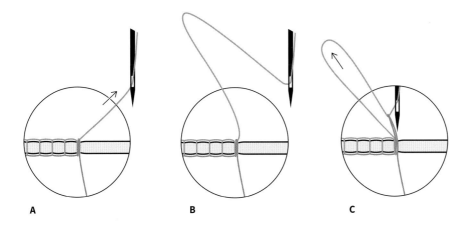

A   B   C

Stopping

1. When reaching the end of a line of stitching, add a few more right on top of the last ones. Then, with the needle up, move the quilt away from the needle about 4″-6″, so there is a tail coming from the quilt to the needle. **fig. A**

2. Use a finger to hook the thread between the quilt and the needle while keeping a firm grip on it. **fig. B**

3. With the thread still hooked on a finger, return to the last stitches of the quilting. Take one complete stitch—the needle should go fully into the fabric once, then back out—and tug on the thread. This pulls up the bobbin thread! Pull the bobbin thread completely up, and snip both the top and bobbin threads. **fig. C**

8

BUILDING BLOCKS

Before we can start creating custom quilting together, we have to learn to make some designs. These are eight of my favorite and most-used designs that can be used on their own as all-over designs if you like.

Now, this may surprise you, but I actually don't really use that many designs. Truly! I know that you are sitting reading this book (I assume you're sitting. Maybe you're standing, lying… running?) and thinking to yourself, "Of course she says that. She is trying to make me feel better so that I buy her book." Honestly though, before I thought of this concept, I thought I was going to have a hard time coming up with enough designs to fill an entire book. That's why this one isn't filled with pages and pages of different designs. The fact is, you just don't need (and probably won't ever use!) that many either. But, I make up for it by being really good at quilting the designs I do use frequently.

By knowing how to use each design in the best place, you create the ability to make the quilt shine and that is what I want to teach you. Think how some of the best dishes at a restaurant are made using just a few simple ingredients. Quilting, just like cooking, doesn't need to be complicated, but it does need to be well executed.

That's why I think you will be successful with this book if you haven't with many others packed with 101 different designs. You'll succeed by learning how to use variations of each design…and by not telling too many people just how few designs you used. Of course, I have blown that last one myself now, but maybe we can keep it just between us?

I get away without using very many designs because I combine the ones I do use in many different ways. We're going to get to all those combinations later, but first things first.

Let's start with some math.

There are eight different designs. Nineteen different combinations. Seven different shapes within which to use the combinations. That's 1064 different ways to quilt a quilt.

See? That's how we are going to get away with only using eight designs.

But back to our basic eight. These are designs I use again and again and again… and again 1061 more times. They are versatile, fun and awesome looking.

I'll introduce them one at a time, building in complexity a tiny bit as we progress through this chapter. If you are new to free-motion quilting, I promise that practice makes perfect. So let's learn these designs, practice them a couple of times (let's face it, quilting quilts is way more fun than practicing designs, so don't feel like you have to practice too much), and then we are going to get to custom quilting in no time.

Ready? Go!

Let's Get Things STRAIGHT

What can be easier to learn than a straight line? Let's start here. I'll be showing you three ways to quilt straight lines which can be used to create some amazing individual designs. I'll tell you my favorite later, but try all three and see which method you prefer.

Best For: Borders

THE WALKING FOOT

Straight Lines (also called Piano Keys) are one of my favorite designs to use in a border, particularly if the border has extra fullness or is a busy print. When the border has extra fullness, it is easy to have some extra fabric in between each line and ease the fabric through the border. With busy prints, it is a simple design that won't take away from the fabric but still looks great!

The first method I'm showing you is using a walking foot. Before beginning to practice this method, have the walking foot attached or engaged. Some machines have a built-in walking foot, but most offer a separate foot that needs to be attached. A walking foot pulls the fabric from the top in sync with your feed dogs pulling from the bottom. This helps keep your quilting even and feeding through the machine at the same rate.

It can still be difficult to keep lines running straight over large distances by using just the tools listed here. But, rather than marking every line, you can mark a line every 4″ or so to cut down on marking but still provide some straight reference lines to follow.

PROS / Easy to keep the stitching even and the lines straight.

CONS / Requires changing the foot on the machine, switching to the one being used for free-motion quilting. Using one also requires lots of manipulation of the quilt to get the Straight Lines sewn in the desired direction.

1. Mark the first line of quilting using a marking tool of your choice (see page 12). I use a ruler that has both horizontal and vertical markings so I can be sure that I am making this first line square with any piecing on the quilt. Sew along the marked line. **fig. A**

2. There are two options for what to do next:

IN LARGER SPACES, or when quilting lines that are more than 3″ apart, mark all of the Straight Lines first, then go back and sew along all those marks. **fig. B**

IN SMALLER SPACES, or when quilting denser lines, use one of the tools that probably came with the sewing machine (such as a presser foot or an adjustable guide bar) to keep the lines straight and even. Run the edge of either of these along the last line of stitching to ensure evenly spaced lines. **fig. C**

A

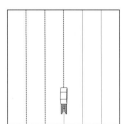

B

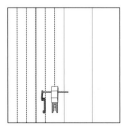

C

MAKE YOUR MARK

The second method is to use marking tools and rulers to indicate the stitching lines, and simply sew over them using the free-motion quilting foot. Because marking tools are not very expensive, I suggest keeping a few to hand and trying out each one on every quilt top somewhere near the binding edge. Depending on the type and color of the fabrics you are using, you may find you have a different preference for the particular marking tool that you decide to use on each one.

PROS / **No need to change feet, quick and easy quilting.**

CONS / **Difficult to keep lines straight.**

1. Mark every Straight Line. It is tedious but it will be worth it in the end! **fig. A**

I lied when I said that you need to mark every line. I like to mark every line to keep crisp, Straight Lines in my quilting. However, if you prefer a more organic look, straight-ish lines might be what you're looking for. In this case, feel free to quilt lines without marking!

2. Stitch on the marked lines in Step 1. Try working both horizontally and vertically, as some quilters find it easier to keep lines straight working in one direction over the other. It is helpful to work relatively quickly as this prevents wobbles in the quilting that can be caused by stitching too slowly. **fig. B**

A

B

KNOWING THE RULES

Rulers are my favorite method for quilting Straight Lines. I can get crisp, Straight Lines without having to change feet or having to turn my quilt in all directions to get Straight Lines in all directions. Look for a ruler with ¼″ markings running the long way across the ruler and as many lines running the short way as you can find—my favorite rulers have those ¼″ spaced lines running in both directions.

PROS/ No need to use a different foot for free-motion quilting and straight-line quilting, easy to keep lines straight, little marking needed.

CONS/ Specialty foot required, which is not included with most sewing machines.

1. Hold the ruler with your thumb and forefinger, making an "L" shape. Keeping half your hand on the ruler and the other half on the quilt will prevent the ruler from moving. **fig. A**

Only stitch in the area between your thumb and forefinger when you're using the ruler—this prevents the ruler from moving, which could lead to wavy quilting lines or broken needles!

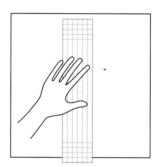

A

2. Run the edge of the foot along the edge of the ruler. Keep the foot snug against the ruler, but don't push too hard against it— pushing too hard makes the ruler difficult to hold in place. **fig. B**

The edge of any side of a ruler foot is a ¼″ away from the needle. Keep this in mind when you are aiming for a certain spot on your quilt—the ruler needs to be a ¼″ away from where you want the stitching to be! This can take a while to get used to.

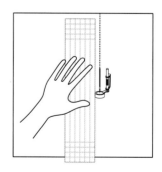

B

3. To keep lines perpendicular, always keep one of the horizontal lines on the ruler aligned with the seam of the space being filled or the edge of the quilt itself. **figs. C & D**

4. Rather than marking each line of stitching, use the lines on the ruler to keep the spacing even. If the lines are meant to be 1″ apart, then measure ¾″ away from the free-motion quilting foot with the ruler. Remember, this measurement plus the ¼″ between the outside edge of the foot and the needle, creates lines that will be 1″ apart.

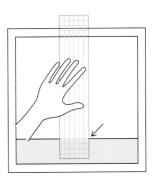

C

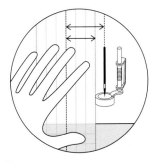

D

Going off the GRID

You can also use straight lines to create grids. While I consider them a building block all on their own, they are certainly straight lines. A grid is also sometimes called a cross hatch. I usually space my cross hatching between ½″ and 1½″ wide, depending on the space I want to fill. If I am filling a space larger than the ruler I am working with, I mark my grid rather than relying solely on the lines of my ruler. This helps to keep everything straight, square and even.

Best For: Backgrounds

GRIDS

Basic Grid

These instructions are for making a 1″ Grid.

1. Place the ¾″ line of the ruler on the edge of the area to be quilted. Stitch a line 1″ from the edge of the quilting area with your ruler foot moving along against the edge of the ruler. **fig. A**

2. After quilting the first line, stitch along the perpendicular edge of the space you are filling (or off the edge of the quilt if stitching the Grid at the edge of the quilt) until reaching 1″ away from the first stitching line. Remembering to offset by ¼″, align the ¾″ line of the ruler with the first line of stitching, and stitch a parallel line 1″ away from the first. **fig. B**

Even if I've pre-marked my grid lines, I still like to use the ruler lines to add an extra level of just-to-be-sure.

3. Once the space is filled with vertical lines, repeat Steps 1 and 2 to fill in the horizontal lines. Use the short lines on a ruler to ensure that the second set of lines is square with the first.

Don't worry about partial squares. If you put a 1″ grid in an 8½″ space, the last space is only ½″ rather than 1″. I just let this happen and don't worry about it.

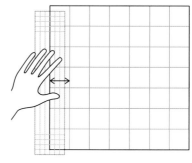

A

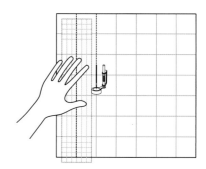

B

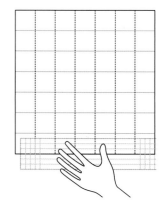

C

Diagonal Grid

Whichever method you chose for making your Straight Lines, you can also stitch them diagonally in order to create a cross-hatch design.

1. First stitch diagonally from one corner to the other to create a perfect 45° angle to use as a reference for the rest of your lines. Stitch on each side of the first line, repeating the process in Steps 2-3 of the Basic Grid (see facing page) to create evenly spaced lines.

2. Stitch diagonally in the other direction from corner to corner, and repeat Step 1 to finish your Diagonal Grid. This is an easy and elegant filler! **fig. A**

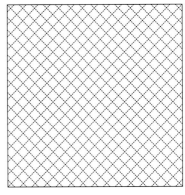

A

60° Diagonal Grid

1. Using a ruler with a 60° line marking (most rotary cutting rulers have two 60° lines on them), align this 60° line with the top of the space you are filling. Mark a line along the edge of your ruler to indicate this angle.

2. Stitch along the marked line from Step 1, and again on both sides of it using the same method you used for our Basic Grid (see facing page). This will create evenly spaced lines.

3. Mark a 60° line using the same method as in Step 1, only this should be a mirror image. If your ruler doesn't have two 60° lines, you can create this mirrored angle by flipping your ruler upside down and using the same ruler line as you used in Step 1.

4. Stitch along the marked line from Step 3, then repeat Step 2 to create a 60° Diagonal Grid. **fig. B**

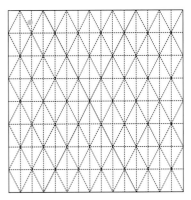

B

As Fancy as a

FEATHER

A long Feather in a wide border is a great way to fill borders both beautifully and quickly. Feathers are one of the fastest shapes to quilt and can dramatically step your quilting up a notch. They are also perfect for adding some elegance or a more traditional look to your top.

Best For: Borders: 6"-10"

FEATHERS

 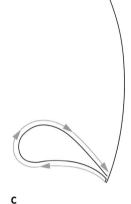 

A   B   C   D

1. Start at the point that will be the top of the Feather and stitch a gentle "S" shape down the quilt, equal to the final length of the Feather. This creates the spine. **fig. A**

2. Make a teardrop shape at the bottom of the "S" shape. **fig. B**

3. Echo the teardrop shape about ⅛" away from the perimeter of the teardrop from Step 2. When quilting this echo, keep the distance between the two as narrow as possible while still looking even. I recommend ⅛" but your may prefer narrower or wider. Practice each shape, to find a comfortable distance. **fig. C**

Echo quilting is when you outline a previously quilted shape at a specific distance away.

4. Create the shape of the next teardrop, starting at the point where the first ended. Keep each barb along the spine that same teardrop shape with a nice rounded curve and always coming back to the same point where the prior shape ended. **fig. D**

The most common problem people have when quilting Feathers is not keeping the barb shapes rounded. Each barb should curve back towards the spine before touching the teardrop shape below it.

E

F

G

H

5. From the point where the second barb hit the first, echo back outside the barb the same distance away as in Step 3. **fig. E**

6. Repeat Steps 4 and 5, working up the spine. Once at the top, stitch back down to the bottom of the spine on top of the original stitching, ready to begin the barbs on the other side of the spine. **fig. F**

_____

If I am stitching a really long Feather, I stop and break my thread at the top and start again at the bottom, rather than stitch all the way back down.

7. Stitch a new teardrop shape on the bottom of the second side of the spine, then echo ⅛″ outside that first line of stitching. **fig. G**

8. Build up the barbs on this side of the Feather in the same way as the first. **fig. H**

_____

I'm often asked, "What do you do with the top of your Feather?" The honest answer? I've never quilted the top of a Feather on an actual quilt. Mine tend to either go off the edge of the quilt or end at a seam or line. So don't worry too much about your top, but if you wish to make one, it can be as simple as another teardrop shape.

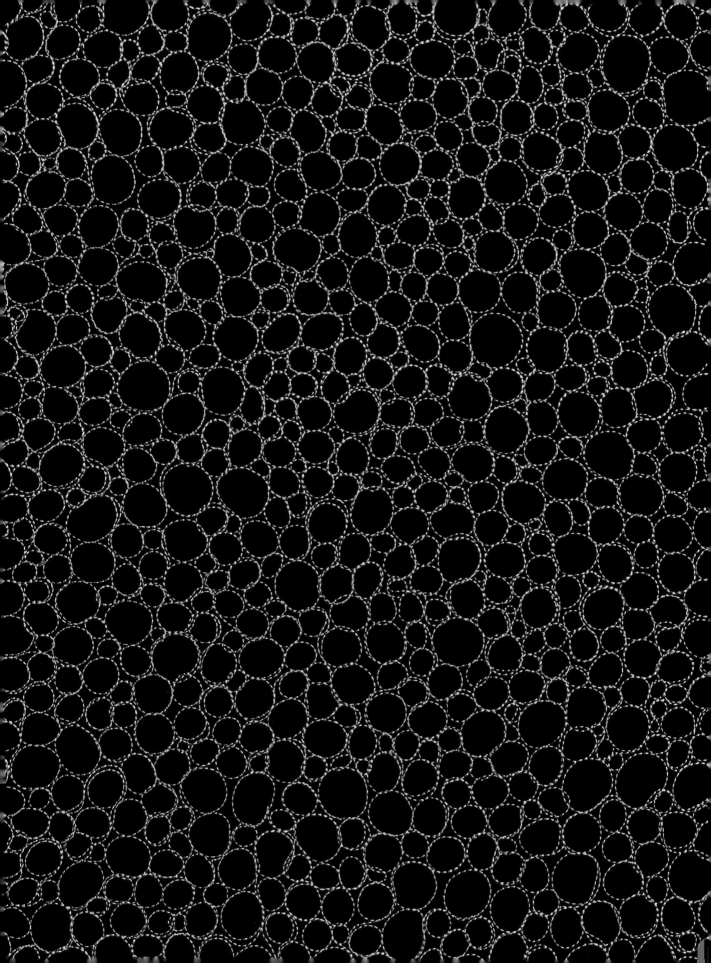

BUBBLES
BUBBLES
BUBBLES

Best for smaller spaces where you want dense quilting. Bubbles are great for making spaces around them pop! Densely quilted Bubbles next to less-dense quilting look great. Bubbles take forever to quilt, so I like to keep them in smaller spaces.

Best For: Smaller Spaces

BUBBLES

A

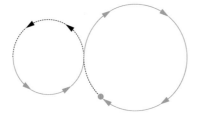

B

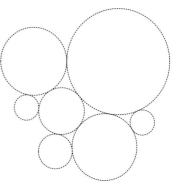

C

1. Start stitching a circle, moving in a counter-clockwise direction. End the circle where it will touch the next circle, indicated here with a blue dot. Your first Bubble! Note that sometimes, getting to the point where the next Bubble will start requires some overstitching on part of a previously stitched circle. Just try to keep the lines of stitching directly on top of one another. **fig. A**

2. Stitch another circle. Overstitch to the point where the next Bubble will touch, indicated here with a blue dot. Don't try to make the circles all the same size. This design is most effective when a bunch of different sizes are grouped together. **fig. B**

3. Keep adding Bubbles in this way, varying the size of each as desired, and fill in all the space in the quilting area. **fig. C**

When filling large spaces, don't stress too much about where to go next. See an empty space, then fill it! You can always backtrack, or fully start and stop to go back and fill empty spaces. In general though, I tend to work from one side of a space to another so that I don't have to do either of those things.

BUBBLE ROW

A

B

C

1. Start on an edge, indicated here with a gold dot. Stitch a circle in a counter-clockwise direction, returning to the starting point. Continue stitching over the top of the previous line of stitching (indicated here with the blue stitching line), until reaching the point opposite, where the second circle will start (indicated here with a blue dot). **fig. A**

2. From the finishing place of the first circle, continue on, making a figure-eight shape. Once again, stitch a complete circle, then continue on top of the previous stitching (again, indicated here with the blue stitching line on the second circle) until reaching the point opposite where the next Bubble will touch (indicated here with a gold dot). **fig. B**

3. Continue making circles in a figure eight motion to fill the quilted area. **fig. C**

_____

If you are making a Bubble Row to fill an actual row of quilting, make sure that the circles don't quite touch the top or bottom of the lines they are between—this will keep the Bubbles looking circular, rather than letting the top and bottom lines flatten their appearance.

Diary of a Young SWIRL

Swirls can be very flexible because they look just as beautiful when they are stitched very small as they do when they are 3″ or even larger. Swirls are my go-to background fill around other designs, piecing, and appliqué. I do find that they can get a little tedious, so I try to adjust their scale depending on how large a space I am filling. With this process, they don't take forever to quilt.

Best For: Medium Spaces

SWIRLS

A

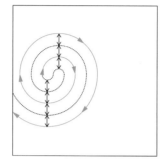

B

C

1. Starting on an edge (not in a corner), stitch a Swirl in a counter-clockwise motion towards what will be the center. When coming back towards the starting point, keep the arc of the Swirl close to the edge of the starting point—if the Swirl were to fit in a circle (indicated here in green), the circle would be touching that edge. **fig. A**

2. Swirl back out from the center in a clockwise movement (indicated here in blue). Try to keep the spacing between each line as equal as possible. Keep following the Swirl all the way around until coming to the edge of the quilting space, or what I call, 'hitting something'. **fig. B**

3. Stitch along the edge of the quilting space—this will either be in-the-ditch or off the edge of the quilt—the same distance away as was established in Step 2. Stitch an echo (see page 30) around the entire Swirl until coming to the edge of the quilting space again. **fig. C**

Every Swirl needs at least one echo, but it can easily have more. I usually aim for two to four echoes, but sometimes I do even more. The more echoes quilted around a Swirl, the more the Swirls appear to be overlapping one another. Adjusting the number of echoes is a great way to vary the appearance of your Swirls!

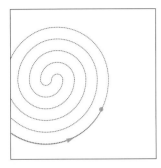

D

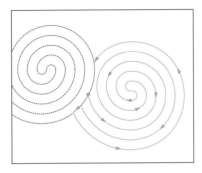

E

F

4. Backtrack along the last echo to the starting point for the next Swirl (indicated here in blue). Use backtracking to avoid starting Swirls in a corner. **fig. D**

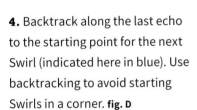

Backtracking is when you stitch right on top of another already stitched line of quilting.

5. Repeat Steps 1-4 to create a second Swirl (indicated here in blue). This time, when following the Swirl until 'hitting something' as in Step 2, that shape will be the first stitched Swirl. Backtrack along the edge of that first Swirl until the second reaches the desired circumference. **fig. E**

6. Continue making Swirls. If there are weird spaces that don't fit a full Swirl, use additional echoes or partial echoes (indicated here in blue) to fill those spaces. **fig. F**

Uniform density is important for quilting Swirls. Your eyes catch spaces with less-dense quilting more than they can identify wonky Swirls and echoes. If you find you have an open space and don't know what to do, simply add echoes!

CLAM

Bake

Clams are an elegant dense filler design. Kind of like
a mash-up between a Swirl and a Feather but with
a bit more kick. They involve a lot of backtracking
which makes them slower to stitch, so I recommend
using them in smaller spaces for high impact.

Best For: Smaller Areas

CLAMSHELL

A

B

C

D

1. A Clamshell starts with a teardrop shape. Starting at the pointy part and working in a clockwise direction, stitch the teardrop shape, ending at the same point as the beginning. **fig. A**

2. From the pointy part of the teardrop, make an echo around the shape, indicated here in blue. Again, the echo should start and stop at the same point. **fig. B**

3. Repeat Step 2 to echo the teardrop shape as many times as desired. I recommend a minimum of two echoes, but often use many more. Just be mindful that the more echoes, the denser the buildup of thread will be near the starting and end point. **fig. C**

4. From the ending point of the first teardrop, make a second teardrop off to the side (indicated here in blue). Vary the stubbiness of each teardrop shape in this design to add interest. This will make some of the first teardrops a little longer and slimmer while others are shorter and rounder. **fig. D**

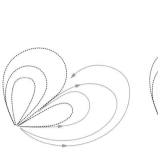

E

F

G

5. Echo the second teardrop. Note that it is not necessary, or even desirable, to stitch down to the starting point again. Only echo until the line of stitching touches the side of another Clamshell, then swirl the stitching back around to create the next echo. This reduces the density of thread. **fig. E**

_____

Pay attention to where the third teardrop will start when ending the final echo around the second one. I usually want to start between teardrops one and two, so end the echo where they meet.

6. Build the third teardrop and echo that shape too. **fig. F**

7. Continue to create and echo teardrops. Try to face the teardrops in as many directions as possible— not all pointing up. Also try to build a new teardrop in between two existing teardrops rather than building them into open space. In Figure G, I have shown you how I might go about repeating eight Clamshells. Notice the variety of directions mine are in.

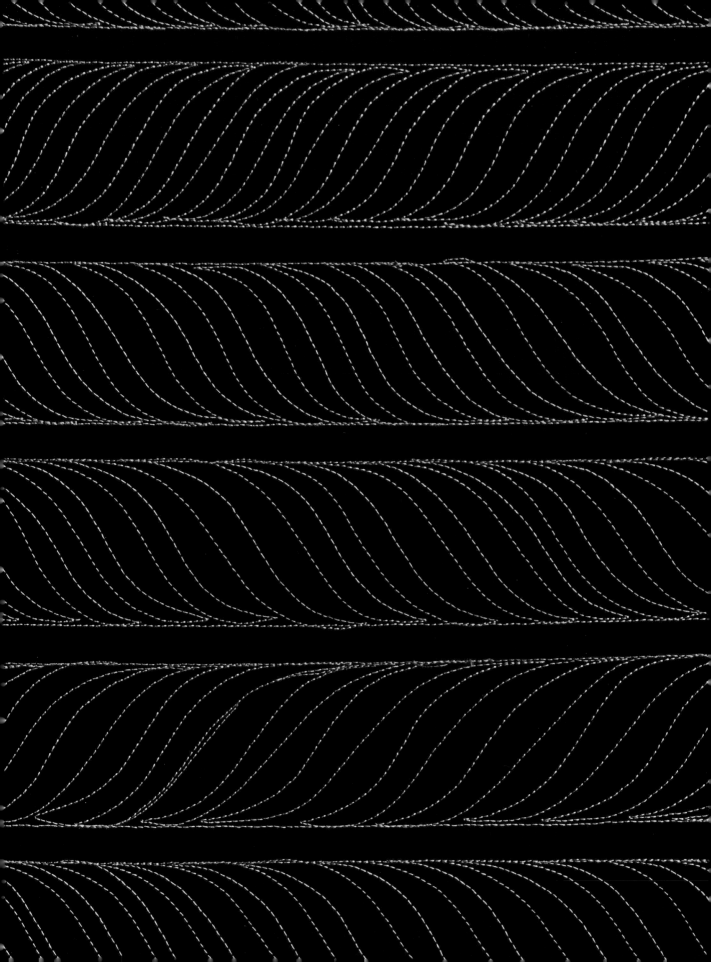

Doing the
WAVE

Waves are great for densely filling an area of sashing or between straight lines. They have just enough movement to keep them from being super-boring to look at, but are simple enough that they don't distract from the piecing in a quilt. I'm not gonna lie. They can be tricky to get the hang of, but keep at it and you'll get there!

Best For: Narrow Borders
1" - 4"

WAVE

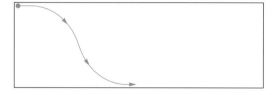

A

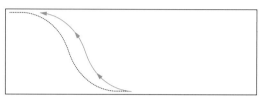

B

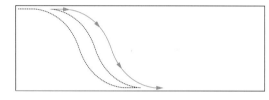

C

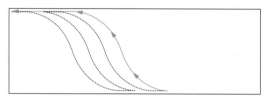

D

1. To practice, draw or sew two horizontal parallel lines about 3″ apart. Start near the inside edge of the upper line, indicated here by a blue dot. Working left to right in a sweeping downward motion, quilt a gentle "S" shape, flowing out from the starting point and almost meeting the inside edge of the lower horizontal line. The line should slope more diagonally, rather than straight up and down. **fig. A**

2. Repeat the same shape from Step 1, this time in reverse, working in an upwards motion from right to left. Stop near the inside of the top horizontal line from Step 1, maintaining the distance between the two sloping Waves.This design flows best when there is lots of stitching along the top and bottom lines, the more each wave can flow into the top and bottom the smoother it will look. **fig. B**

3. Repeat Step 2, but when returning to the inside of the top horizontal line, backtrack to the original starting point in Step 1 to connect the Waves on the top edge. **figs. C and D**

I find it much easier to fill in my initial shapes, then go back to fill the first section, rather than starting with the smaller lines. Having the longer lines to echo, helps to keep the flow of the design even as it gets smaller.

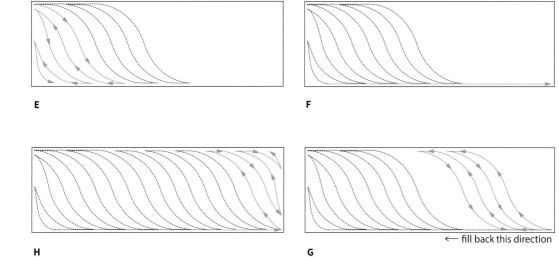

E

F

H

G

← fill back this direction

4. Fill in the area to the left of the first stitched line from Step 1. Keep repeating the Wave shape to fill the area, making the Waves shorter as necessary. **fig. E**

5. Backtrack to connect the Waves along the inside bottom line all the way back to the furthest right edge of the quilting area, past the Wave from Step 3. **fig. F**

6. A "gentle S" may get a bit wonky while you are stitching and it may not look right (this certainly happens to me!). To fix this, give up on the bad curves, stitch along the top or bottom for a couple of inches, and quilt a nice new curve. Then, echo the brand-new Wave backwards towards the wonky curve. **fig. G**

7. When reaching the end of the quilting area, finish it off in the same way as the start of the line from Step 4. **fig. H**

Winning a
RIBBON

Ribbon Candy is possibly my most favorite design to quilt. I see an empty area of sashing or space that's about 2″ tall, and all I want to do is quilt Ribbon Candy in it. It is less densely quilted which can really make it stand out and makes it perfect for drawing your attention to a specific area. A variation of the same movement is the Continuous Curve. See? Two for One!

Best For: Large Areas

RIBBON CANDY

A

B

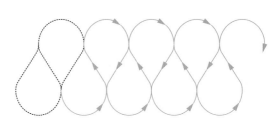

C

1. Ribbon Candy also starts with the teardrop shape from Clamshells, but it is a bit chubbier (it's candy, after all). Start the top of the teardrop at the position indicated by the blue dot. Create the shape in a downward counter-clockwise movement. It should be large enough to fill about ⅔ of the space being quilted. The teardrop should start and stop at the same point. **fig. A**

2. From the point where the first teardrop ended (back at the top), start a new teardrop shape, this time working upwards in a clockwise movement. Stop stitching at the point where the teardrop from step 1 begins to curve into a circular shape, roughly in the middle of that shape. **fig. B**

3. Continue making teardrops facing in alternating directions until the space is filled. **fig. C**

_____

I try to make my Ribbon Candy just barely smaller than the space it is filling. This way, the top and bottom of my Ribbon Candy stay round, and they aren't being flattened out by the straight edge of the space. If my aim is a little off, and my Ribbon Candy gets a little big, I'm still within the lines!

CONTINUOUS CURVE

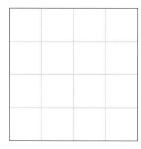

A

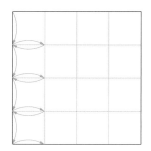

B

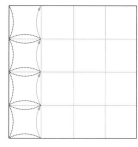

C

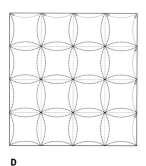

D

1. Create a Grid using the Grid technique (see page 30). This grid can be any size but I recommend a Grid between 1″ and 3″. **fig. A**

2. Start in the top left corner of the Grid, and work down the first column, making a slight curve from corner to corner of each grid square. Work down, right, left, down, right, left, down, right, left, down, etc., until reaching the bottom. **fig. B**

My general rule is that if my grid is less than 2″, I quilt the curves freehanded. If my grid is larger, I use a curved ruler.

3. Work back up to the first corner, curving slightly from Grid corner to Grid corner. **fig. C**

4. Repeat Steps 2 and 3 until reaching the farthest edge of the quilting area. Stitch curves along the right edge of the last set of squares. Then, stitch curves along the tops of all the squares on the top edge of the space, working left to finish off your continuous curve. **fig. D**

Building

COMBINATIONS

Now that we know how to make a few designs, let's see how many ways we can combine them! If you're trying to figure out what to quilt on your quilt and you get stuck, overwhelmed, or just feel like playing a fun game, we've got something great at the back of the book. Use the spinner to choose which combination to use, then pick design playing cards to decide which designs to use in that combination. Take the thinking out of your quilting and get right to the fun part!

What is Custom Quilting Anyway?

This book is called *The Building Blocks of Free-Motion Quilting: Combining 8 Easy Designs into Knock-Out Custom Quilting*. You know, in case you forgot which book you were reading.

But what exactly is this custom quilting?

Custom quilting is using the quilt top itself to inspire the quilting. It's not an "all-over" design, or, to say it another way, not just one design quilted over the entire quilt with no consideration being given to the piecing lines. In custom quilting, we use different designs in different places to create something… custom. Usually different pieces of the quilt will be quilted differently, often with different colors of threads to match each individual fabric. Custom quilting is the type of quilting that makes you stop and look twice, it is something beautiful in itself, not just thread holding three layers of a quilt together.

Examples of Effective Custom Quilting

Maybe you are not quite sure what the difference is yet? Here are some examples, where you can see how introducing some simple separation of spaces, creates different areas to stitch one of our eight building block designs within or around. It's that simple to go from an all-over single design to custom quilting, just by stitching up a contrasting design in an adjacent space.

Improv Lines

Best For:

Spaces you'd like to fill with just Straight Lines but don't have a lot of piecing lines to follow. Also great when you have a large space where you want the clean, modern look of straight lines, but you don't have the patience to try to keep the lines perfectly straight over the entire space without a lot of marking.

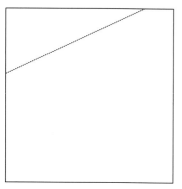

1. Sew a Straight Line from one edge to an adjacent edge, creating a triangle in the corner.

2. Using the first line as a guide, fill the triangle with Straight Lines approximately ¼″ or the width of your presser foot, apart.

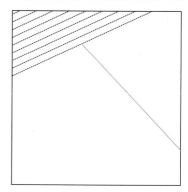

3. Section off another area of space with another Straight Line connecting to the one from Step 1.

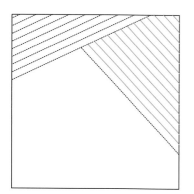

4. Repeat Step 2 to fill this space with lines as well.

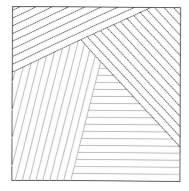

5. Continue to section off areas and fill them with Straight Lines. Be sure to vary the orientation of the stitching within each area to prevent the sections from blending together.

Variations

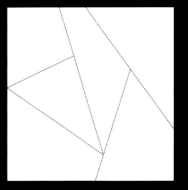

*Looking for a less-dense design?
Use only the dividing lines, and
don't fill in the spaces after they
are sectioned off.*

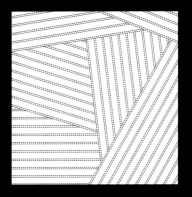

*Try varying the spaces between
fill-lines! Stitching two very close
lines instead creates an extra
dimension in your quilting.*

Open Space Split

Best For:

Medium-sized spaces. This is one of my favorite techniques when I have a square between 6˝- 10˝ to quilt. Split the space and quilt away. If repeated, it is possible to create some really interesting secondary designs with the split as well!

I most often use this design when dividing a square space diagonally from corner to corner, so that is how my directions are written.

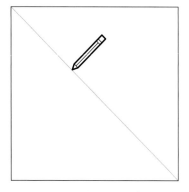

1. Using a marking tool (see page 12), draw a diagonal line from one corner to the other.

2. Stitch two lines ¼˝ away from the line in Step 1, one on either side of the drawn line.

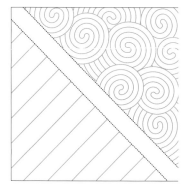

3. Fill each side of the stitched lines with a different design. Choose designs that contrast well so that the split is very noticeable.

When I'm choosing two contrasting designs, I like to think about the density and the swirliness of each one. I want to have two designs that either have different densities or two designs that have different swirliness. Swirliness is the amount of curve in a design—Bubbles and Swirls have high swirliness—while Straight Lines and Grids have no swirliness.

Variations

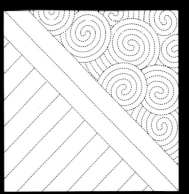

Rather than marking the first diagonal line, stitch it. This gives the open space we want, but we can skip the marking!

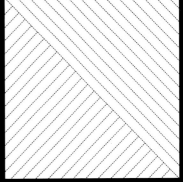

Instead of two different designs, try straight lines in different directions.

Lines and Designs

Adding depth and interest to an area. The straight lines tend to pop to the foreground, while the design areas move to the background, creating really interesting textures.

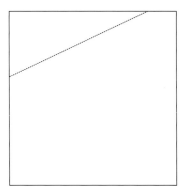

1. Sew a Straight Line from one edge of the space to be quilted, to an adjacent edge, creating a triangle in the corner.

2. Using the first line as a guide, quilt several Straight Lines at the same angle as the one from Step 1. I usually quilt at least four additional lines... maybe a lot more.

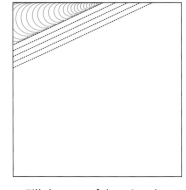

3. Fill the rest of the triangle created by the Straight Lines with a design. I chose the echo of Clamshell but without the first teardrop. Who says you need to use the entire motif?!

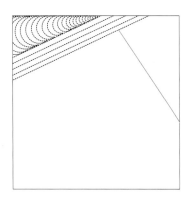

4. Section off another space with a Straight Line just as with Improv Lines (see page 58).

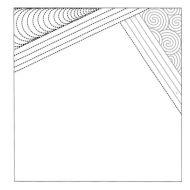

5. Using the line from Step 4 as a guide, repeat Steps 2 and 3.

6. Repeat until the space is fully quilted. Consider filling an entire section with Straight Lines rather than adding another design to create a strong linear look.

Variations

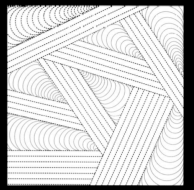

Rather than using a new design in each space, try using the same design again and again. This creates a more uniform look to the quilting.

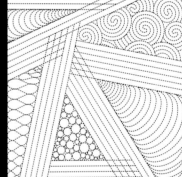

Try crossing some of the dividing lines in the corners of your sections rather than stopping when you touch a line. This creates even more texture.

Design Overlap

Best For: Use this combination when mainly using one design, but you don't want the effect to be too boring either. Great for creating a crack or a vine through an area of quilting.

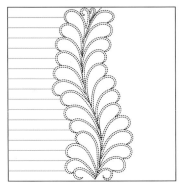

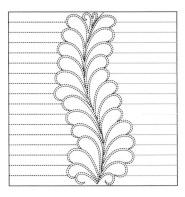

1. Quilt the foreground design. In our example, I use a Feather. But it could be a chain of Swirls or Ribbon Candy or Clamshells.

With this type of combination, we are trying to make it look as though one design (the foreground) is sitting on top of another design (the background).

2. Fill in the background design on one side of the foreground. Choose a design that contrasts with the foreground. It works well if the background is slightly denser than the foreground and quilted at a much smaller scale.

3. Fill in the background of the second side of the motif from Step 1.

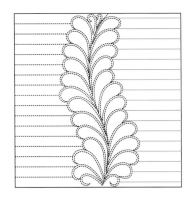

If you are using Straight Lines as a background design as I have, be sure that each line looks as though it continues underneath your foreground and it doesn't jog at the foreground. To prevent this, when I'm stitching the second side of the background, I line up a ruler with the previous line of stitching on the opposite side of the foreground design and mark that line of quilting to be sure that they will align perfectly.

Variations

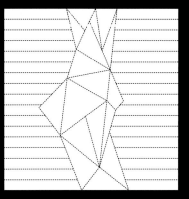

Use randomly quilted Straight Lines as your foreground motif to create the appearance of a crack through the quilt.

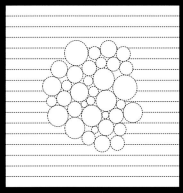

Rather than having a long thin line of foreground splitting the space into two distinct sections, group a motif in a section and quilt Straight Lines around the entire shape.

Design Vine

Best For: Splitting the space. Great for large spaces that benefit from two different fills. Perfect for a dense fill around a block or appliqué and a less-dense fill through the background spaces. Also great to prevent getting bored filling a large space with the same design that will have to be stitched and stitched and stitched....

1. Stitch a design to split the entire space to be quilted.

Always quilt the motif that will appear as though it is on top, first. For this design, I quilted the Feather first. Because the rest of the stitching will be around this first shape, it will appear as though the background stitching continues underneath the Feather.

2. Stitch a contrasting background design on one side of the design from Step 1.

3. Choose a second background design for the other side of the design from Step 1. This should contrast with both the previously quilted designs.

If you are going to the bother of quilting three designs, you want everyone to know that you did! Create contrast by varying the density or the swirliness of the motif (see page 58).

Variations

Feathers aren't the only things that you can use as a vine! Here, I used a line of large circles to split the space.

You don't always have to make Feathers on both sides of the spine. Here, I put Feathers on one side, and I did a simple echo on the second side, before filling in the background.

Corners of Awesome

Best For:

Creating focus on a central motif. Adding corners directs the eye towards the center of the space on which they are added. I use them often when I have an appliqué or a pieced block with a lot of negative space around it.

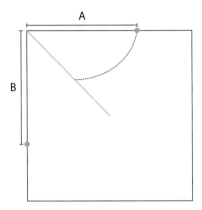

1. Mark a 45° line starting from a corner where the design will begin and extending towards the edge of the quilted corner area to fill.

2. Using a curved ruler, stitch from the edge of the block to the marked line. To decide where the line should go, move the ruler around in the space to audition placement.

Don't have a curved ruler? Instead, find a dinner plate, cup or something with the curve you are looking for. Use a marking tool (see page 12) to trace around the item, and stitch on top of the marked line.

3. Measure the distance between the corner of the block and the point where the stitching of the previous line started (A). Measure and mark this same distance down the other side of the corner (B) and make a note of this measurement to ensure that the other three corners will be the same shape.

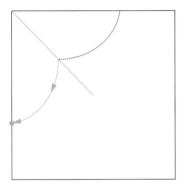

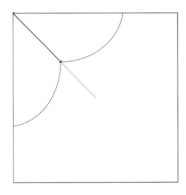

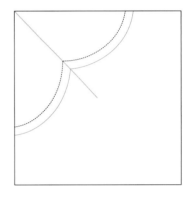

4. Using the curved ruler or utensil once more, stitch from the end of the previous curve to the point marked in Step 3.

5. Measure the distance on the diagonal from the corner to where the curves meet at the diagonal line. Record this measurement for use later.

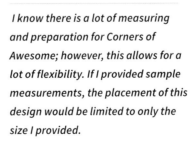

I know there is a lot of measuring and preparation for Corners of Awesome; however, this allows for a lot of flexibility. If I provided sample measurements, the placement of this design would be limited to only the size I provided.

6. Depending on the density of the quilting through the rest of the quilt, echo the full curve using either a ¼″ or ½″ spacing.

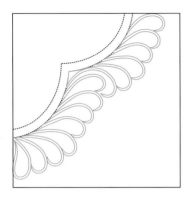

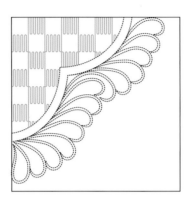

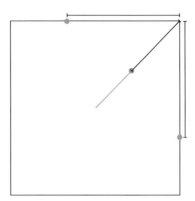

7. Use the echoed line from Step 6 as a spine for a row of Feathers.

8. Fill the inside of the corner with a Grid design.

In my stitched sample, I filled every other grid space with a dense simple coil-like design to create some extra texture.

9. Move to the next corner and mark the two ending points of the first curved lines using the measurement from Step 3, then mark the diagonal measurement taken note of in Step 5.

10. Stitch the curves starting at the diagonal point marked in Step 9. See how re-using all these measurements keeps all the corners exactly the same? Repeat Steps 6-8.

11. Repeat Steps 9 and 10 for the remaining corners.

Variations

Rather than stitching a Grid inside each corner, try using Straight Lines following the right angles of the perimeter. This creates an even stronger frame around the center.

For a more modern look, skip the Feathers altogether. Instead, use an extra echo of the curves to create space between the Corners of Awesome and the center of the quilt.

Grid Sampler

Best For:

Medium-sized spaces, between 6″ and 12″. Using in any larger area makes it difficult to keep the lines straight and the Grid square. The linear Grid always provides great contrast to Swirlier piecing.

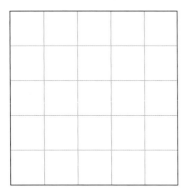

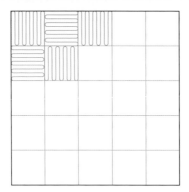

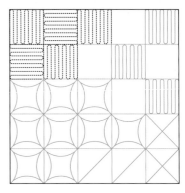

1. Stitch a Grid throughout the desired area to fill. Try to complete as much of the Grid as possible before starting to fill the squares as this will stabilize the quilt and make it easier to keep the lines straight.

2. Fill several Grid squares with a design. Vary how many squares are filled with each design, but it should be a nice chunk. Try not to make a distinct pattern with the same design being mindful that the same one doesn't fill a full line or create a diagonal one. This should be just a random fill of designs.

3. Continue quilting with a variety of fill designs until the entire Grid (or most of it) has designs in it.

Variations

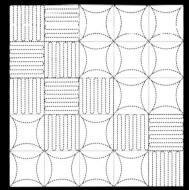

Try using only two designs to fill the Grid. This creates more cohesion in the overall pattern while still providing pockets of different textures.

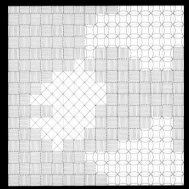

Use larger fill areas of each design in the Grid. Rather than each filling only five or six squares, have each fill 10 or 20 or 30 squares! This creates large swaths of one texture, with another large texture next to it. Definitely best for very large spaces!

Trip Around the World

Best For:

Medium-to-large spaces, where you want some design cohesion, but you don't want to quilt the same thing over and over again. Draws the eye to the center, so it works great for quilts or blocks with a central motif.

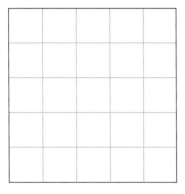

1. Sew a Grid over the entire area that will be quilted. A 1″ quilted square works well, but larger ones will also work.

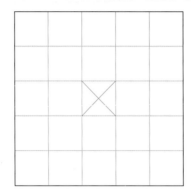

2. Find the center square in the Grid and start there. Fill the center square with the first design.

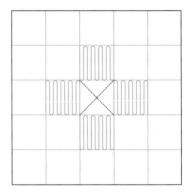

3. Choose a second design, and quilt it in the squares above and below and to the left and right of the center square.

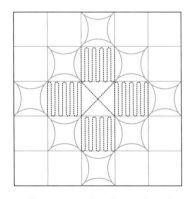

4. Create another 'round', using a third design. Each round creates an on-point square encompassing the previous round.

When creating Trip Around the World combination, use at least three designs. If only two are used, the effect will be more like a checkerboard rather than the rounds intended in this design.

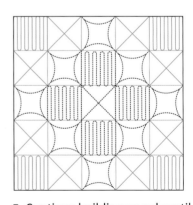

5. Continue building rounds until all the squares are filled. On the outer rounds, you will run out of space for a full round, so just fill as much as possible.

Variations

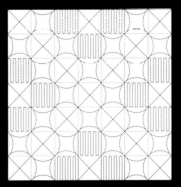

This variation is 'The Reverse Trip Around the World.' Rather than starting in the center and building designs in rounds, start with an "X" shape, crossing in the center square. Continue in rounds on each side of the "X" until all the squares are quilted.

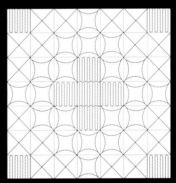

Rather than doing a single round of each design, try two (shown here) or three rounds of each design. This works particularly well in larger spaces, and it makes the rounds of each design more prominent.

Fade

Really, really large spaces—Use this combination over an entire quilt top, especially one pieced with the same-sized squares, because the Grid doesn't have to be marked first. Score!

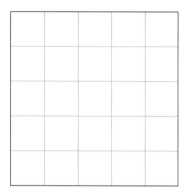

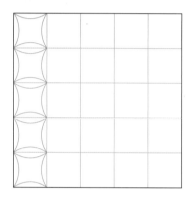

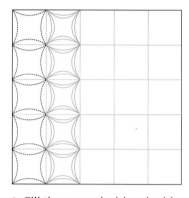

1. If there isn't a Grid already pieced on the quilt top, begin by stitching one in the area to be quilted. A good quilted square size is between 1″ and 2″ for this design.

2. Fill the first column of the Grid with a Continuous Curve design.

3. Fill the second with a double Continuous Curve. To create this, first stitch a regular Continuous Curve, then stitch a second set in the same column. The second set should have more of a curve but is not quite an echo. The starting and ending points of both curves should be the same.

Depending on the size of your grid squares, a triple Continuous Curve may be all you have space for in each grid. If you have a larger grid, you may want to go up to five or more Continuous Curves in each square at the densest filling.

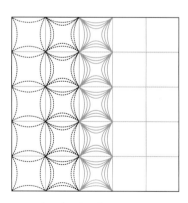

4. In the third column, stitch a triple Continuous Curve.

5. In the next column, begin reducing the number of curves, so repeat Step 4, then 3, then 2, back up again until the Grid is full!

Variations

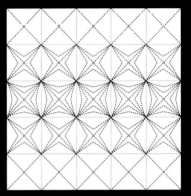

Try a shape other than a
Continuous Curve! Here, I used
an "X" shape in each square.
This is an easy way to get an
interesting different look out of
the same design.

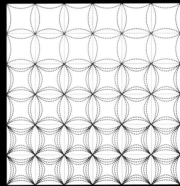

Try reducing how frequently the
number of Continuous Curves
changes. Here, I used two rows
of single, two rows of double,
and two rows of triple.

Bubble Space Split

Best For:

Medium-sized spaces. This is one of my favorite techniques when I have a space between 6˝ and 10˝ square to quilt—split the space and quilt away. It seems a little fancier than the Open Space Split. The row of Bubbles adds a touch of class, like a strand of pearls. I tend to choose between this and the Open Space Split depending on the look I am going for— the Bubble Space Split is just a touch more traditional.

1. Mark a diagonal line from one corner of the area to be quilted to the other.

2. Stitch two lines ¼˝ away from the marked line from Step 1, one on each side of the drawn line.

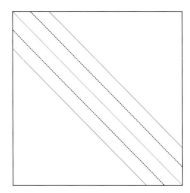

3. Stitch a line ¼˝ away from the lines stitched in Step 2. This creates four stitched lines, spaced ¼˝, ½˝, and ¼˝ apart.

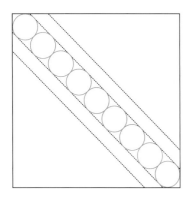

4. Fill the center ½˝ space with a Row of Bubbles.

5. Fill each side of the stitched lines from Step 3 with a different design. Use ones that read differently from each another. Think about the swirliness (see page 58) and the density of the designs to help with this.

Variations

Forget the Bubble part of the Bubble Space Split, and try another design! Here, I used squares, which are pretty similar to Bubbles and are just as easy to quilt.

You can use the split for something other than a straight diagonal line. Here, I created an "X", but you could also try a curved line or a straight up and down line.

Stripes

Best For:

Large spaces that need lots of texture and where it is important to provide structure. Perfect for quilts with piano key borders— just continue the stripes off the borders and into the quilt!

0. Step zero! There are a few things to think about before starting this design.

- Decide on the width of the stripes even before selecting the fill designs. Sometimes having all the lines the same size is appropriate, other times, it is better to vary.

- Leave a ¼″ to ½″ stripe of unquilted space between each quilted one. This provides much-needed separation. Skipping this causes the fill designs to blend together, losing the effect of the stripes.

- Choose contrasting fill designs that vary in either Swirliness or density to fill in the stripes. If the stripe widths are similar, the contrast between fill designs is even more important.

- If you are quilting stripes of varied widths, the contrast between the fill designs is less important. The width variation helps create the necessary contrast.

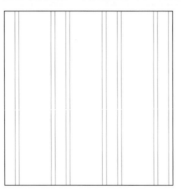

1. Mark the lines rather than rely on rulers or the foot of your sewing machine. This is particularly important when the stripes cover a large area.

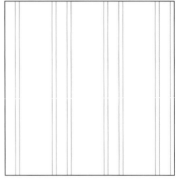

2. Start stitching the marked lines from Step 1, working from one side of the quilt top to the other.

3. Fill the stripe. Always quilt the lines on both sides of a stripe before stitching the design itself. This provides stabilization.

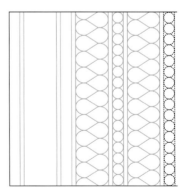

4. Continue across the quilt, stitching the marked lines on each side before going back with the fill. Keep going until all the stripes are complete.

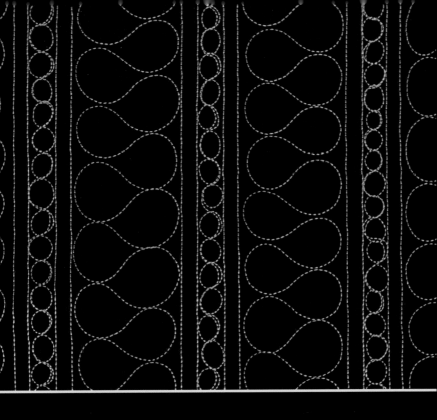

Variations

When using similarly wide stripes, choose designs that contrast with one another well! Here you can see that the less-dense Ribbon Candy looks great with the denser Wave fill.

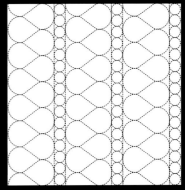

Here is one not to try! I skipped the open space between the filled stripes. You can see how the lines just blend together rather than creating the more structured look of stripes with the open lines. If you are putting in the effort to create stripes, be sure that they are visible… which means remembering to leave in those open space

LONGARMING INSTRUCTIONS: If you are quilting on a longarm, think about the direction of the stripes before you load your quilt. Stripes are easiest when they can be done in one long stretch, so they should run parallel with the bars of the frame. This might mean that your quilt should be loaded sideways!

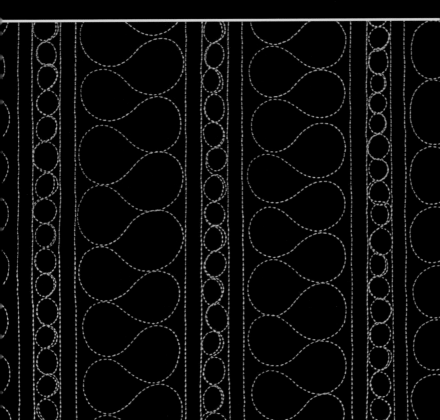

Design Overlay

Best For:

Creating contrast. This is one of my favorite opportunities to use contrasting thread, adding color and extra interest to a large area of open space. The Design Overlay combination is also great when you need to keep a consistent density, but you have a plan for a design that doesn't have consistency. Stitch a bottom layer of consistent background, and use the second design more randomly as the foreground!

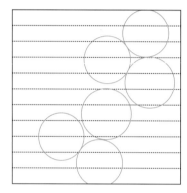

1. Unlike the Design Overlap, here the background design is quilted first. Choose one that is even in density throughout, to keep the background looking like a background fill—you want the foreground design to be the focus. To aid in this, consider switching the thread color as I did in my quilted sample on the facing page.

2. Quilt the foreground design. This should stand out from the background, so be sure it contrasts with that design. To achieve this, consider varying the shape, size and density of the quilted design for the foreground.

Variations

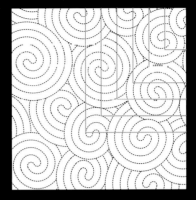

Switch the swirly and straight designs. Here, the Swirls became the background and Straight Lines the foreground. This creates a geometric look, despite the Swirls being underneath the Straight Lines.

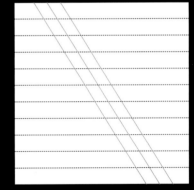

Sometimes, it doesn't take much to create interest with this technique. Try a group of Straight Lines with one chunk of lines going in a different direction! This is a great way to break up space over a large area while maintaining a modern look.

Part II: Building Combinations   81

Thread Color Change

Best For:

Creating subtle or stark contrast or creating highlighted areas. Use greatly varying hues for an obvious look, or use a just-barely-different thread color to create a subtly highlighted area.

My quilted sample on the facing page has three thread colors—two neon yellow-greens and a dark grey. The two neon colors create a slight highlight of the brighter yellow. It is just enough for you to think, "Maybe there is something going on there?" but not enough to be obvious. The dark grey is a significant contrast in thread color to the neon, but blends into the background when compared to the other two thread colors.

1. Start quilting with the first color. The first thread used to quilt appears to sit on top of the next thread color. For this reason, I recommend using the higher-contrast thread first.

2. Fill in the rest of the quilting with a second thread color. Alternatively, go crazy and put in a third, fourth, or fifth color after the second!

Variations

One of my favorite ways to use Thread Color Change is to use different colors for the focal design and for the background fill. Here, I used one color for the circles and a different color for the background fill. Even with just a subtle thread color change, the circles will stand out just a little bit more.

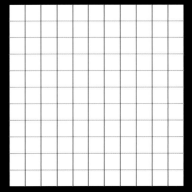

Try using different colors for the lines in each direction of a Grid— one for the horizontal and one for the vertical. This can mimic the look of shot cotton so that, depending on the direction from which the quilt is being viewed, a slightly different color will be more apparent.

Design Blend

Best For:

Large spaces where it makes sense to have a different design on each side of a space. I love to use this on quilts with appliqué or sashing, where I need a design that is easy to work around those small, tight spaces. But I also want a seamless transition into the open.

1. Start quilting the first design. Fill the area up to the point where the first and second designs will begin to blend.

The more space you leave for the transition between the two designs, the smoother the transition will be. I recommend 8˝ for the transition at the very minimum, but between 12˝ and 15˝ will give your quilting a smoother blend between the two designs.

2. Begin the transition to the second design. I recommend repeating the mantra "more design one than design two," as you progress through the transition area.

Here, I used Swirls as the first design and Straight Lines as the second. A word of caution: If you are planning to use similar designs for your blend, quilt the linear design after the Swirly one. Otherwise, it can be difficult to tell where the second design should fit.

3. Continue quilting the designs while moving across the quilting space. Gradually include less and less of the first design and work in more of the second design instead. Change your mantra to "more of design two than design one," as you sew across before finally transitioning into using only the second design.

Variations

Choosing two similar designs, such as Swirls and Bubbles, will help create a smooth transition more easily. It doesn't produce as much contrast, though, so be sure to select the two shapes carefully.

Rather than choosing two different designs to create a transition, try blending different densities of the same design. Here, I moved from a dense Swirl into a looser one, achieving the same transitional effect.

Design Meld

Best For:

Large spaces where a distinct change between two designs is desired. Great for having a denser design around more intricate piecing, then moving to a linear or less-dense design in more open spaces. Also great to fill a large space without getting bored with quilting the same design over and over again—use this technique to switch things up.

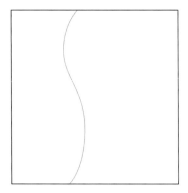

1. (Optional!) Draw a quick line with an appropriate marking tool (see page 12) to indicate approximately where the design should change. This helps us visualize when it is time to change designs. This is especially important if using this combination for a large space.

I usually don't want a straight line between designs here—I like to use a curvy line as my marked line. A straight one tends to look too rigid for this combination.

2. Stitch the first design, filling up the space to where it will change. If you've drawn a line in Step 1, use it as just a general guide, not a hard one that the design is not to go past under any circumstances. As shown in the illustration above, some designs go slightly over the line and some are not quite meeting it.

When working from an edge of an area, linear designs don't seem to work well as the first design, but they work great as the second! They are easy to work 'under' other designs, but it is hard to find a good place to stop them when they are the foreground design.

3. Fill the rest of the space with the second design. Work the design into all the spaces to really make it look as though the first design is floating on top of the second.

Variations

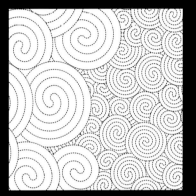

Try using one design but with noticeably different scales. Here I used a large-scale Swirl first, and a smaller as the background. I always like to use the larger scale as the foreground, as less dense quilting always tends to stand out more.

Rather than a smooth marking, I tried a jagged line between the designs. This gives more valleys for the second to fill and creates a more random look. When filling in that second design, be sure to get into all the spaces between the first to create a great effect.

Part II: Building Combinations **87**

Full Random

Best For:

Any-sized space where there needs to be a reasonably even texture throughout the quilt, but you don't want to get bored quilting the same design over and over and over and over again. Despite the many individual designs used in this method, the texture in the end is even, because the designs are each used evenly. This makes it great for background fill.

1. Start quilting the first design. Use larger or smaller chunks of each design depending on the size of space being quilted. Usually, I recommend a section about 2″ to 4″ square.

2. Quilt the second design, keeping the chunks of each about the same size as one another.

While I do try to make each design chunk the same size, I aim to vary their shape quite a bit—some might be more circular, others long and skinny, and others just weirdly shaped. This approach balances consistency with interest.

3. Continue filling in the area to be quilted, creating stitch close-to-equal-sized chunks of each design. In my quilted sample on the facing page, I used four designs, but feel free to use as many or as few as appropriate.

Once again, if you are using a linear design, like the Straight Lines I used in my quilted sample, it is easier to quilt on all sides of the space that the lines will be within, before quilting the lines themselves. This provides a place to end each line and travel down to the next one, which is tough to accurately visualize when you are ending lines into open spaces.

Variations

This variation has three of the four designs used in my stitched sample. I eliminated the Straight Lines, which changed the outcome of the quilting significantly. Without those Straight Lines, the quilting has a much more even texture to it.

Rather than using chunks of design, try evenly filling space with two or three designs. This creates even density and texture, making it great for a background fill. Use this when a simpler quilting design is preferred but the thought of quilting just one design over and over makes you a little crazy.

Grouped Random

Best For:

Really, really, really big spaces! Perfect for quilts with SO MUCH negative space. This is my go-to solution for quilts that have such large swaths of negative space, that I have no idea what to do with them. This technique creates large sections of different textures, creating an interesting background without too much thought (and no marking!).

1. Choose the first design and start quilting over a large section of the quilting area. How large that will be depends on the scale of the quilt and the total area being filled. The larger each chunk can be, the more noticeable the variations in texture.

At this point, you might be thinking, "Isn't this exactly the same as the full random design, only with bigger design chunks?" Well, you're right. However, it gives such a different look that it needed to be more than just a variation. I quilted this over a queen-sized quilt with a lot of negative space throughout and used sections of each design that were two or three feet square.

2. Fill large sections of space with different designs. I usually recommend at least three designs, each contrasting with one another.

Create contrast with varying swirliness rather than density in this technique. Quilting such large areas of each design means that a variation in density can easily create puckers, cause the quilt to not lie flat, and... well, let's just not do it and not find out.

Variations

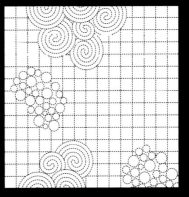

Try smaller chunks of a few designs with the rest of the space filled with a linear one. Here, the Swirls and Bubbles look as though they are sitting on the Grid, adding little spots of texture.

Grids are notoriously hard to keep straight over a large space. This technique helps to break up those long lines.

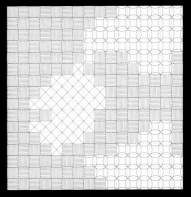

This probably looks familiar—I used this as a variation of the Grid Sampler. But it is also a Grouped Random—large groups of the same design being used to create different textures but within a Grid.

Spiral Design Combine

Large spaces where the background needs to have movement. This technique creates a swirling effect, which is great for drawing your eye to the center of the Swirl.

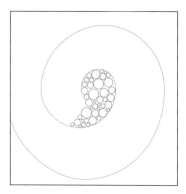

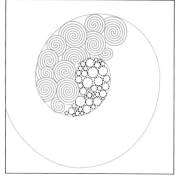

1. Mark a spiral that fills the quilting area, indicated here with the gold line. Larger spaces should have more open spirals, whereas in smaller spaces these should be tighter. Starting in the center of the spiral, begin quilting the first design, using the marked spiral as a loose guide for where the design should stop.

If you are working on a domestic sewing machine, starting in the center of the spiral is easy! However, on a longarm, starting in the center can be annoying if the spiral is larger than the workable space on your longarm. If you are a longarmer, see my tip on the facing page.

2. Stitch a second design, continuing to use the marked spiral as a guide for the space that each design should fill. Don't try to make the marking an exact barrier, but rather use it as a general guide.

3. Keep stitching designs around the spiral, using the marked one as a guide for each section. As you are filling in the areas of the spiral, whatch that the same designs don't accidentally touch on both sides of a marked portion of the spiral. It is surprising how often this wants to happen, particularly near the center.

Variations

A square spiral (that is, a spiral that follows a square shape rather than a circular one) gives a similar effect, drawing the eye to the center. The square adds a more structured look and lends itself to more geometric designs, such as Straight Lines.

What other shapes can you think of to use as your markings? Here, I used stripes. When we learned Stripes, I emphasized that there should always be a line of unquilted space between each fill so that the stripes are visible. However, Spiral Design Combine is a large filler, so skip those empty spaces and fill each design right up to the next.

LONGARMING INSTRUCTIONS: Rather than working from the center and around, on a longarm it is much easier to start at the top and work downward. Start with a design at the top, and use the marked spiral as a guide for when to change designs. This achieves the same effect overall, we just go about it in a slightly different way.

Improv Shapes

Best For:

Medium-to-large spaces that need lots of texture. Creates an almost-pieced effect, which is great in large, open spaces.

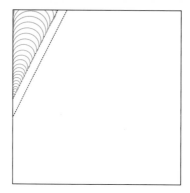

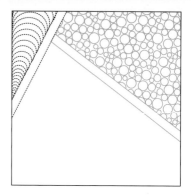

1. Sew a Straight Line from one edge to an adjacent edge, creating a triangle in the corner. Echo the sewn line, indicated here with a blue line. Depending on the scale of the quilting, this echo should be between ¼″ and ½″ wide. Keep the echo density just slightly larger than the density of the fills—this helps to make the lines really stand out.

It doesn't really matter when you echo the first line—you can do it right after you make the first line or after you've filled the space with a design. However, I find that I'm less likely to forget the echo if I stitch both at the same time.

2. Fill the closed space with a design.

3. Quilt another straight line to close off a second space. Echo the line, and fill the space with another design. Try not to have two spaces with the same design touching each other.

4. Continue splitting the space, echoing and filling in with designs until the space is full.

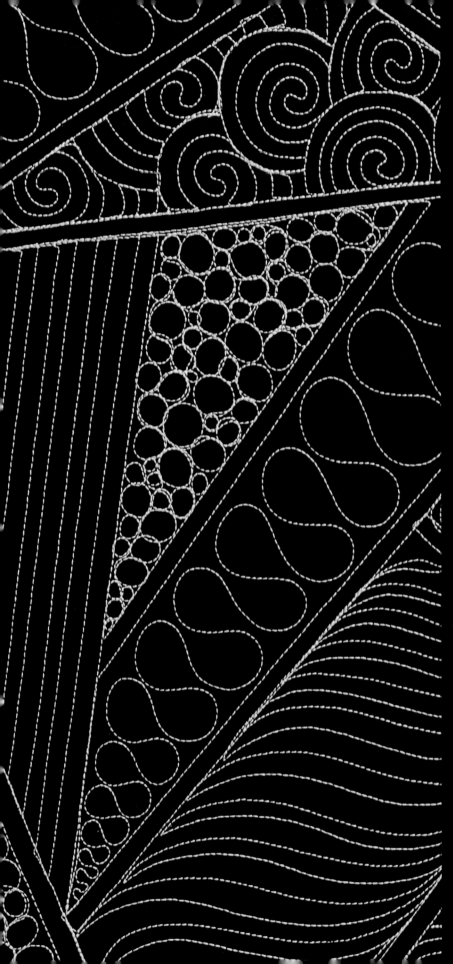

Variations

For a more even look, try using the same design in all the spaces. This gives the illusion of the echoed lines sitting on top of one large background fill—a different and very cool effect.

This is one of my favorite ways to quilt tops that have lots of different shapes and fabrics in the piecing—just quilt every piece differently! In this case, I usually don't make an echo when I quilt it in the piecing. The different fabrics provide the separation without my having to artificially make a separation with an echo.

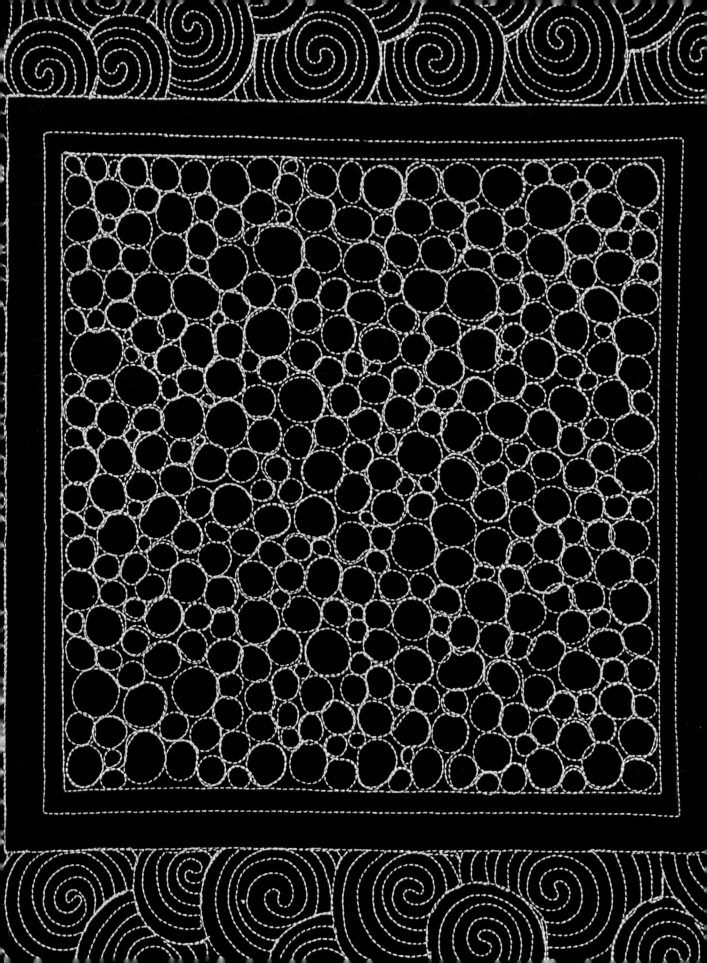

Part III

Using

SHAPES

For quilt tops that don't have a lot of piecing lines to follow, I like to create shapes with my quilting first, and then fill them accordingly. This is a great technique to have in your quilting toolbox, especially for tops that have background blocks and pieced blocks repeating, leaving symmetrical areas of negative space you want to call attention to. Using a repeated shape can also direct your quilting throughout the top.

Making Shapes

Shapes are a great way to emphasize the parts of our quilts that we want to show off. Create a shape around it and ta-da: emphasis. We can use many of the techniques we learned in the Building Combinations section in conjunction with some simple shapes to create really interesting effects.

While I only show the basic outline of the ways to use each shape, we most likely need more quilting than just this! Always leave a space of unquilted area between the inside and outside—to do this, just echo the shape. I usually fill the inside of my shape with a denser fill that is easy to quilt around whatever weird shapes are in my piecing or appliqué. Then I choose a less-dense or geometric design to fill outside the shape, with a small, unquilted line in-between the two designs. However, you can use any of the design combinations we learned in the Building Combinations chapter to create these shapes!

Examples of the Effective Use of Shapes

Not quite sure what I mean yet? Here are some examples where you can see how including some simple shapes, creates new areas in which to stitch a design, whether those shapes appear in the piecing or not.

Create a shape around it and ta-da: emphasis.

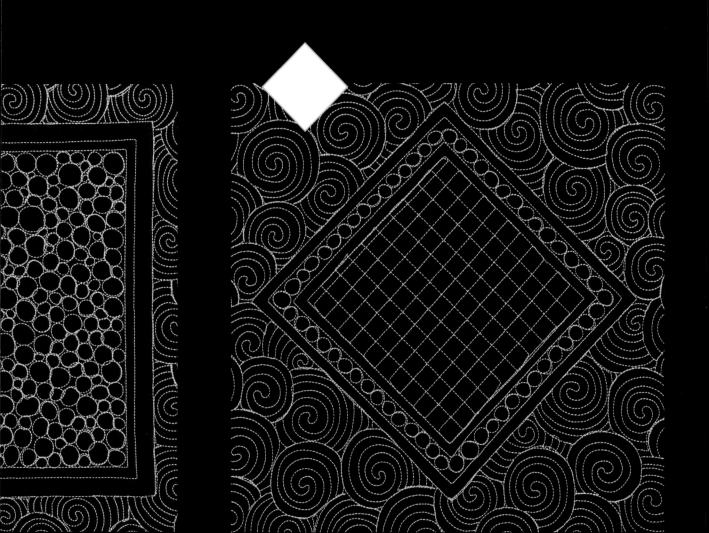

Faux Border

Best For: Quilts without borders, but with negative space around the outside of the quilt. Here and throughout, I will be using illustrations that have grey stars to mimic what the piecing in a top might be and how best to use shapes to break up the top for quilting.

MARKING TIPS: When marking the border, find something in the quilt to use as a reference for the square placement. Don't use the outside edge of the quilt, because this can get slightly distorted through the basting or loading process. By using the piecing as a guide to help the established distances remain identical, the border stays squared up with the piecing.

Borders are easier to mark entirely before you begin quilting. However, if you are like me and often don't have an idea in mind until after beginning, just mark one section at a time. I often use a repeated block in the quilt for this—maybe a border is always 2″ away from the point of the star, for example.

VARIATION ONE: I love having an imposed border appear to go underneath some of the pieced parts of the quilt, rather than leaving it as a true border going around the piecing. This approach adds an extra layer of interest to the quilting. It also provides a place to break up the linear quilting, making it easier to keep those lines straight.

VARIATION TWO: For a more modern look, try having a border on only two sides of the quilt. This divides the quilting area into a large square and two borders; perfect for that Ribbon Candy or Wave fill. This approach is ideal if there are already some offset designs in the piecing.

VARIATION THREE: Borders don't always have to be straight lines! Here, I created a border using Feathers, giving a much softer look. This is a great idea to try if the top has a larger central motif that can be framed by the quilting.

Faux Border

Diamonds

Diamonds

Best For: Emphasizing a specific area of the quilt. Just like the square, this treatment can be used in multiple places throughout the quilt top, or used as a large shape across most of the top.

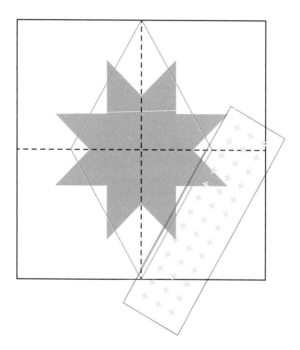

MARKING TIPS: Mark a "+" sign through the center of the area to be quilted, indicated here with the black dashed lines. Using a ruler with 60° markings—most rotary cutting rulers will have these—place one of the 60° lines on the horizontal line of the "+". Mark a line running to a vertical dashed line at the point where the lines of the diamond shape will meet. Repeat this process working in a clockwise direction, to mark the four sides of the diamond (indicated here in gold).

VARIATION ONE: Intersecting the selected shape with the piecing or appliqué in the quilt top, creates a much more interesting look. The key is not to cross over the piecing or appliqué with the quilting. This way, it will appear as though the piecing or appliqué is floating on the surface of the quilting. This is also easy to quilt, as there are many starting and stopping points where the piecing or appliqué intersects the lines of the diamond, once again, providing a chance to make sure the lines of the shape are straight.

VARIATION TWO: Rather than having an individual diamond for each block in a quilt top, try using one large diamond over the entire quilt. This adds another layer of interest to the background, rather than a more expected block-based design.

VARIATION THREE: Try combining the diamond with some of the combinations we learned in Part II. Here, I built stripes out from the diamond. Filling each of the larger spaces with a design and leaving the smaller spaces unquilted, creates the effect of a radiating diamond.

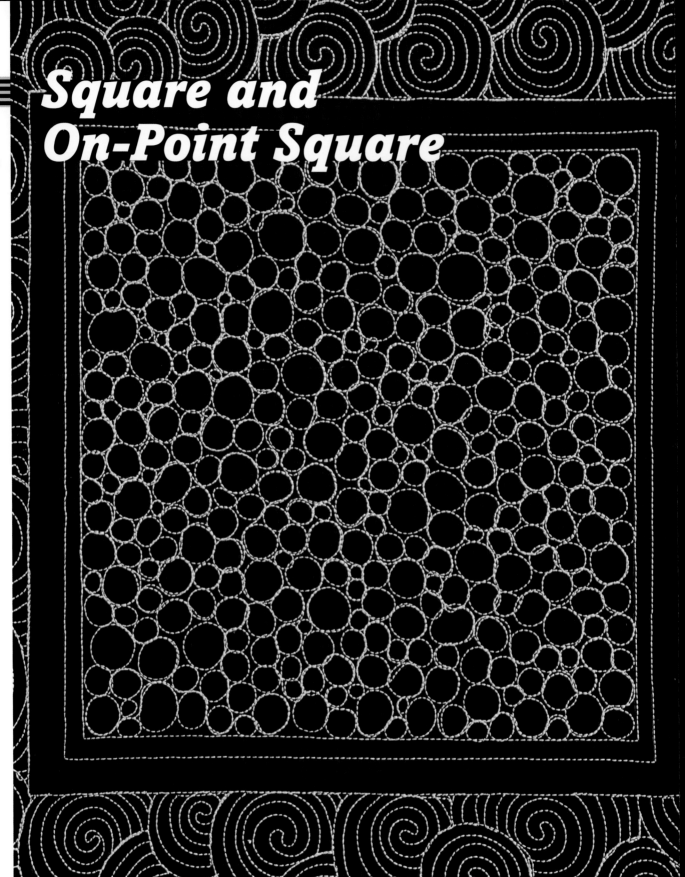

Square and On-Point Square

Square and On-Point Square

Best For: Emphasizing a specific area of the quilt, whether it be appliqué or piecing. This can change the feel of the quilt very easily, so be sure to consider the final cohesive look of the quilt before selecting one of these approaches.

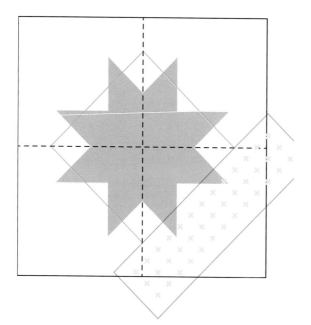

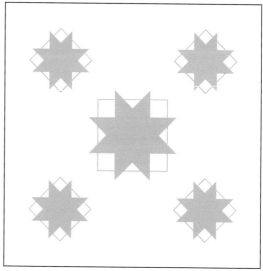

MARKING TIPS: Again, find something in the quilt to use as a reference for creating a square. If you are making a square around a block, use the piecing of the block itself as that reference.

Use a ruler with 45° markings. Most rotary cutting rulers have this line, as do many quilting rulers. Mark a "+" sign, with the center of the "+" in the same spot as you'd like the center of your on-point square to be (indicated here with the black dashed lines). Position the 45° line of the ruler on the vertical line of the "+", and draw a line from there to the horizontal line of the "+". Continue around the "+" until the on-point square is marked.

VARIATION ONE: Guess what I'm going to say for placement here? You got it! Once again, intersecting the quilted lines with the piecing makes for both a more interesting look and results in easier quilting.

VARIATION TWO: Try placing multiple shapes in the same quilt for added layers and texture. Here, I combined a square and a number of on-point squares overlapping one another to create a complex look. The dashed lines shown here indicate where one shape is "under" another and should remain unquilted. This is one of my favorite ways to use shapes because it is so unexpected.

VARIATION THREE: Rather than sticking to perfectly square or perfectly on-point, try a random angle. Start by marking your first line, then use this marked line as your reference for creating the rest of the square. This introduces a modern look to a quilt top.

Circle and Oval

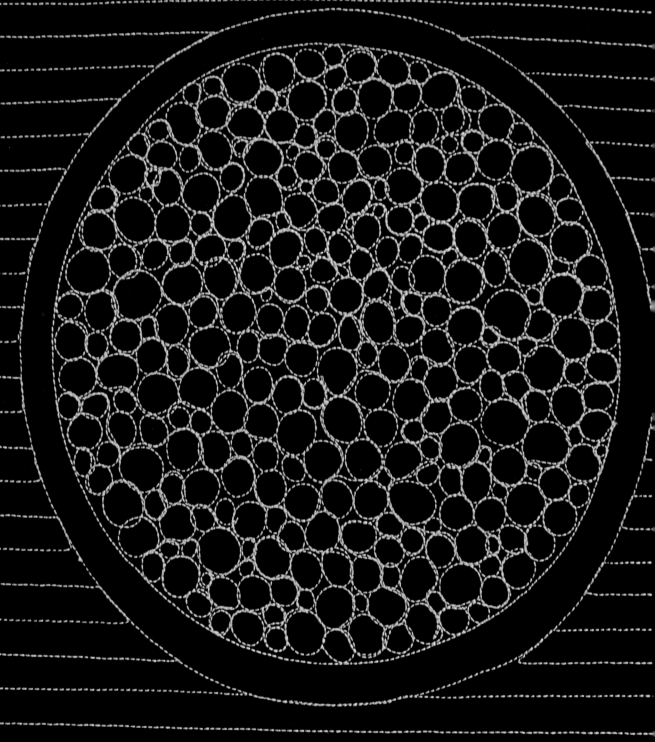

Circle and Oval

Best For:

Emphasizing specific spots on a quilt. Circles create a softer look than the angled shapes we've been talking about so far, and can be a nice contrast to a lot of linear piecing.

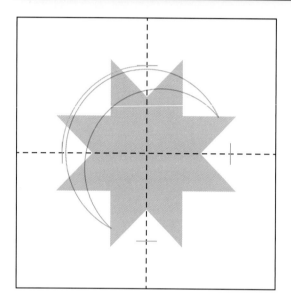

MARKING TIPS: Draw a "+" sign through the intended center of your circle, indicated here by the black dashed lines. If using a full-circle ruler or an object to mark your circle, simply place the center on the center of the "+", and draw around it. If using an arc ruler, as illustrated above, find the diameter of the circle it creates—this is usually printed on the arc itself. Divide that by two, and mark that distance from the center of the "+" on each of the four arms as indicated here in blue. For example, if your arc will make a 10″ circle, measure 5″ away from the center point in four directions. Then, use you arc ruler to connect all four of these markings.

VARIATION ONE: Having the quilted lines intersect with the piecing or appliqué is great for circles and ovals. As with other shapes we have talked about, this creates great interest in the quilting. However, I find I am more willing to have circles and ovals completely encompass a shape rather than intersecting them. I am less willing to do this with other shapes.

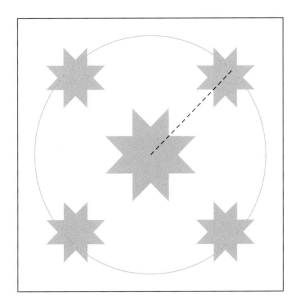

VARIATION TWO: Mark large circles by pinning one end of a long piece of string to the center-point of the circle, tying the other end to a marking tool. Keeping the string taught, use it like a large compass to mark circles of any diameter you like by simply changing the length of the string. Huge circles are great for creating a border-look or tying together a large space.

VARIATION THREE: Try breaking up a circle. Here, I put a quarter circle in each corner of the quilt rather than a full circle through the middle. I marked it the same way as in Variation Two, and it splits up the quilt in an interesting way.

I have a large selection of circular and arc-shaped rulers to help me quilt and mark curves. This makes it easy to get the exact diameter I want. However, if you aren't quilting professionally, you might not want to spend your life savings on a bunch of curved rulers. Look around your house for different circular and curved items you can use to mark—cups, rolls of tape, plates, mirrors—I've even had a student use a turkey platter to mark a large oval!

Using the Piecing

Using the Piecing

Best For:

Quilts with piecing! Shocking right? I use this technique most often in quilts with more traditional settings—that is, quilts with lots of the same or same-sized blocks repeated over and over again. I also use this when tops have any proportional setting.

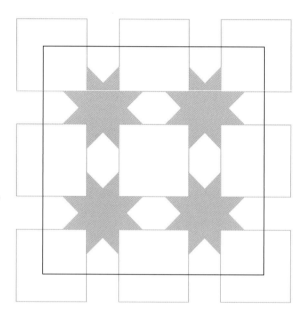

MARKING TIPS: Often, using the piecing equals less marking, particularly when using rulers. Simply align the ruler with one part of the seam created in the piecing and connect it to another seam. When quilting Straight Lines without a ruler, simply use a favorite marking tool and a long ruler to connect some of the piecing to create the desired shapes.

VARIATION ONE: Look for shapes that are naturally created by the piecing. In this example, I saw a square created in the center of the quilt. I used this to show that while there is only one full square in the center, there are also several partial squares around the edges which I could use to reinforce the central one. Also, look for 'incomplete' shapes in the piecing that you might want to complete through the quilting, not just the more obvious full shapes.

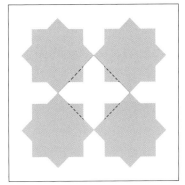

VARIATION TWO: Look for shapes that your piecing can create. Using the same central square as in Variation One on the facing page, there are many other square repeats that are options. These are indicated here in the blue, gold and green lines. The next step is to choose which one to accentuate. There is no right or wrong selection, but I think about the finished look I want to achieve as well as how difficult each shape is going to be to mark and quilt. If I can't decide between a few, I usually go for the easier shape.

VARIATIONS THREE AND FOUR: Look for less obvious shapes. Here, I highlighted an on-point square that appears to slip under part of the piecing. This adds an extra layer of interest to the quilting. Next, I added extra lines—I wanted the quilting to look as though there might be more of it underneath the grey piecing.

Part IV

FINISHING Up

We are soooooooooo close to being done with the quilting, but sometimes we find some problems when we inspect our work. So lets fix them quick so we can enjoy our quilts!

Troubleshooting Your Quilting

ONE OF THREE THINGS CAUSES 95% OF ALL FREE-MOTION QUILTING PROBLEMS:

THE NEEDLE. We talked about needles in the Set it Up chapter, so we know that needles need to be strong enough not to flex as we quilt. If I run into trouble with my quilting, the first thing I do is change the needle—even if I have just changed it. Needles can be sensitive, and it doesn't always take a lot for them to need a change.

THE PRESSURE FOOT HEIGHT. Different machines have different pressure foot settings for free-motion quilting. If you have one that bounces up and down as you quilt, you don't need to worry about this. If you have one that floats at one height all the time you are working, you need to watch this. Your pressure foot should float so it is just touching the top of your quilt sandwich—it shouldn't be putting so much pressure on the quilt so that it becomes hard to move. Also, you don't want to have any gap between the quilt top and the pressure foot.

THE TENSION. You can tell if your tension is off if you are getting loops of bottom thread on the top of your quilt or loops of top thread on the bottom. Tension is easy to set: just remember, "lower the number, lower the knot." If you have bottom thread on the top, it means that your machine is making a knot too high in the quilt—so the knot needs to be lower: lower the tension of your machine.

If one of these solutions doesn't solve your problems, take your sewing machine to your dealer to get some extra help. To get the best help, don't change anything on your machine: leave it exactly as it was when you ran into trouble.

Removing Markings

One of the bummer parts of marking a quilt is that the markings have to come out again. Depending on the marking tool you've used, you have a few options.

MECHANICAL FABRIC PENCIL: I often just let these wear off over time. But if I'm in a hurry to get them out, I'll take a clean, dry kitchen scrubby and scrub at the marking. If I've got a sticky spot, I'll take some Sew Clean (a fabric-specific cleaning spray available at your local quilt shop), spray it on my scrubby, and scrub the fabric with it.

PURPLE AIR ERASE MARKER: These markings disappear over time, and people often think that they are gone forever. Not true! They can come back over time and can be brought back with laundry detergent. I always recommend when you wash a quilt that has been marked with a purple pen, you first wash it with water only: no detergent or fabric softener. After the first wash, wash it as usual.

BLUE WATER ERASE PEN: The proper way to get out this type of marking pen is to completely submerge the quilt in water—I often use a soak cycle in my washing machine with no detergents or fabric softeners. Then I lay the quilt out flat to dry. However, sometimes I am lazy, or I just don't want to get the entire quilt wet, so I take a spray bottle and spray the markings until they are soaking wet. Then I let it dry and spray it again. I do this three or more times to make sure that my markings are definitely out of the fabric.

Blocking

Blocking is done when a finished quilt doesn't lie or hang flat. Don't freak out: just block the quilt. The basics of quilt blocking are to get it wet, lie it perfectly flat, and leave it there to dry. I use a few methods for this, listed here in order from the least work to the most:

1. Lay the quilt on the floor and use a spray bottle to mist the surface. The wavier the quilt, the damper it needs to be. I use this method most often.

2. Put the quilt through a gentle cycle in your washing machine. If the top isn't bound yet, be careful. The friction caused by the washing machine can cause some of the stitching along the edge to come out.

3. Fill a bathtub with enough water to completely submerge the quilt. This is the proper way to do things. I'm not going to lie here though; I've never actually done this.

After any of the three dampening methods, spread out the quilt so that it lies perfectly flat. If needed, I use items around the house to help: heavy books, binders, or whatever else I can find.

If the quilt binding isn't attached yet, trim the top square. If you check whether a quilt needs blocking before you trim or put binding on, the process will be much easier. If blocking many quilts, consider purchasing foam floor tiles that can be pinned into directly to keep the quilt flat while drying. This also protects the floors from the wet quilt. You can get these floor tiles at most larger stores.

GLOSSARY

ARC RULER: A ruler shaped like a crescent moon for marking and quilting curves.

BACKTRACKING: Stitching over the top of a previously stitched line of quilting.

BACKGROUND FILL: A quilting design such as Swirls, Clamshells, or Bubbles that fills in between larger or more prominent designs.

BASTING: Temporarily securing the three layers of the quilt sandwich together so that they stay together while quilting.

CONTRAST: Being strikingly different from one another. In this book, usually used in the context of using two or more designs within a space.

DENSITY: How closely together the quilting is so, quilting stitched closer together is denser than when there are large spaces between the lines.

DESIGN CHUNK: What I call a grouping of the same quilting design in one restricted area.

ECHO: A close and parallel repetition of a previous line of stitching, usually between ¼″ and ½″ apart.

FEED DOGS: Rows of little metal teeth built into a sewing machine under the plate that move fabric forwards or backwards as you sew.

FREE-MOTION QUILTING FOOT: Sometimes called a darning foot. A specialty foot that allows for free movement of the quilt sandwich in all directions.

GEOMETRIC DESIGN: Quilting designs based on straight lines or grids.

MARKING: Drawing temporary lines on a quilt top to use as a reference for future designs.

QUILTING RULER: A ruler in a variety of shapes designed to be used with your sewing machine to guide free-motion quilting. It is often made from thicker clear acrylic than a rotary cutting ruler.

QUILT SANDWICH: The three layers of a quilt ready to be quilted. These layers consist of the quilt top, a layer of batting, and the backing fabric.

ROTARY CUTTING RULER: A ruler designed to use with a cutting mat and rotary cutter. Usually made of a thinner clear acrylic than a quilting ruler.

SWIRLINESS: The relative number of curves in a quilting design. The more curves there are, the swirlier the design is.

TENSION: The balance needed between the pull of the top thread and the bobbin thread in your sewing machine to create an even stitch.

WALKING FOOT: A specialty sewing machine foot with teeth that grab the fabric to help with even feeding.

ACKNOWLEDGEMENTS

Thank you to my sister, Jennifer Kerr, for editing my first draft, and finding 2766 changes; my mom, Ardelle Kerr, for binding all 42 quilt samples, which I was just not willing to do; the Lucky Spool team, for making my book look way more awesome than I ever could have imagined and for making all my scattered ideas make sense.

Get over yourself and just do it.

This is something I have to tell myself often. It is a reminder to stop overthinking, to get out of my head and to just get to work. Just start quilting. Now is the time when I let you loose in the world: the end of the book. So go quilt! Find a quilt top, look at it, decide what you want to quilt and quilt it. Don't think too hard for too long, just go for it. It's going to be awesome.

Then send me pictures :D

Later days,
Kathleen

Spin that Wheel!

As you are practicing or if you are stuck for ideas, use this handy spinner to give yourself a challenge. Cut this out together with the next four pages from the book. Separate the eight Building Block Cards and cut along the dashed white lines. Next, cut out the arrow shape from the back flap of this book. Glue the wheel onto a thin piece of cardboard (a cereal box will do!), cut around it, then use a sharp tool to create a hole in the center of both the arrow and the wheel. Attach a brass fastener through both holes and secure on the back of the wheel. Spin away, blindly selecting the number of Building Block Cards indicated on the spinner to create a quilting design. See, I told you quilting was fun!

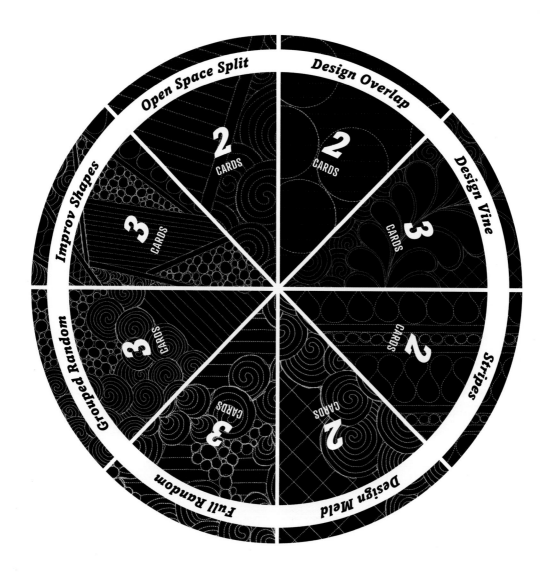

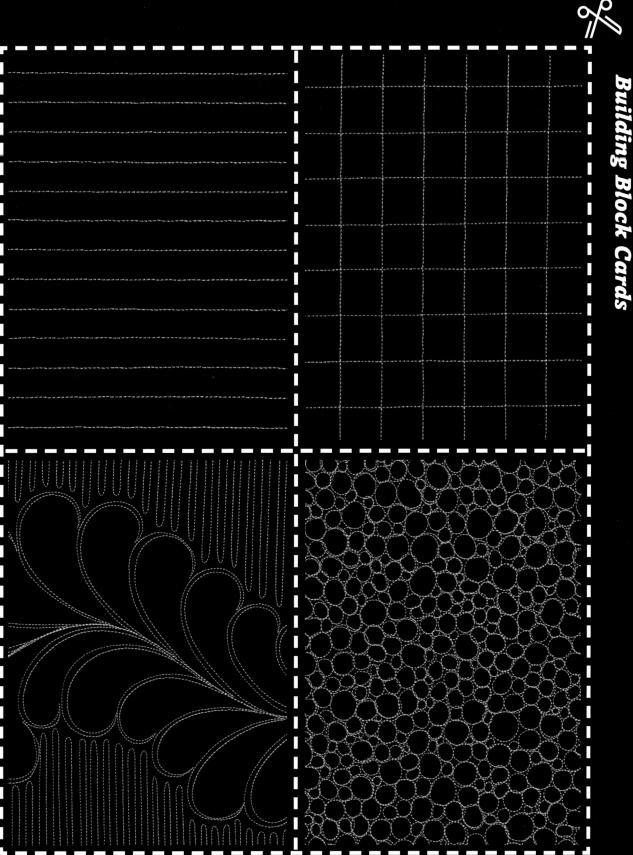

Grid

Using any of the Straight Line methods, create a Basic Grid, Diagonal Grid or 60° Diagonal Grid. Grids work best as the background design and should usually be stitched last.

Straight Lines

Fill an area using any of the three methods for creating Straight Lines. Straight Lines work best as the background design and should usually be stitched last.

Bubbles

Using Bubbles or a Bubble Row, add this design to one area of your quilting space.

Feathers

Integrate a Feather into one area of your quilting space. Feathers work best as the foreground design, and should usually be quilted first.

Clamshell

Don't clam up! Stitch this pattern into one area of your quilting space. Remember: this design is better for smaller spaces because it is one of the more intricate Building Blocks.

Swirls

Get swirly! Quilt some Swirls into your quilting area. You can alter the size of your Swirls depending on whether they will be in the foreground (large Swirls) or background (small Swirls).

Ribbons or Continuous Curves

Stitch some Ribbon Candy into your quilting area. Then maybe go eat some candy. If the area isn't suitable for this design, use Continuous Curves instead.

Waves

Ride the waves and quilt some into your quilting area. Try elongating them to make them a background design if needed.